# NEARBOUND

## AND THE RISE OF THE WHO ECONOMY

Jared Fuller

**NEARBOUND**.COM
**REVEAL**

Copyright © 2024 nearbound.com

All rights reserved. No part of this book may be reproduced, distributed, or transmitted in any form or by any means, including photocopying, recording, or other electronic or mechanical methods, without the prior written permission of the publisher, except in the case of brief quotations embodied in critical reviews and certain other noncommercial uses permitted by copyright law.

Some portions of this book appeared in *The PartnerHacker Handbook*, *The Nearbound Sales Blueprint*, and as articles on nearbound.com and have been edited and used with permission of the authors.

Edited by Shawnie Hamer
Cover art and illustrations by Taiesha Turner


ISBN: 9798880308699

First Edition: February 2024

Printed in the United States of America

nearbound.com is a project of Reveal.

*For Atom & Sophia*

# CONTENTS

ACKNOWLEDGEMENTS ................................................................... i
FOREWORD BY JAY MCBAIN .......................................................... v

## FOUNDATIONS ...................................................................................

    TRUST IS THE NEW DATA ........................................................... 1
    NEARBOUND DEFINED .............................................................. 22

## NEARBOUND MARKETING ................................................. 45

    THE CURIOUS TASK OF MODERN MARKETING ....................... 46
    THE NEW CMO ........................................................................... 51
    SURROUND SOUND MARKETING IN 5 PHASES ....................... 60

## NEARBOUND SALES .............................................................. 83

    HOW SELLING REALLY WORKS ................................................ 84
    THE NEARBOUND SALES BLUEPRINT ...................................... 90

## NEARBOUND COMMUNITY ............................................. 111

    SOCIAL SELLING 2.0 ................................................................ 112

## NEARBOUND CUSTOMER SUCCESS ............................... 129

### TYING SUCCESS WITH THE SERVICING BOWTIE ...................... 130
### FROM BOWTIE TO FLYWHEEL ........................................................ 137
### SUCCESS THROUGH NEARBOUND PRODUCT ........................... 146

## THE NEARBOUND OVERLAY ........................................... 153

### NEARBOUND PARTNERSHIPS ....................................................... 154
### NEARBOUND OPERATIONS ........................................................... 163
### NEARBOUND AND THE RHYTHM OF BUSINESS ...................... 173
### THE NEARBOUND MINDSET .......................................................... 192

# ACKNOWLEDGEMENTS

In the spirit of *Nearbound and the Rise of the Who Economy*, a book that celebrates the transformative power of partnerships and relationships for business, it's fitting to begin by acknowledging the partnerships and relationships that have shaped me into the man I am today—and the man I strive to become.

Naval Ravikant once wrote, "All returns in life, whether in wealth, relationships, or knowledge, come from compound interest." He advised us to "play long-term games with long-term people." These words encapsulate the essence of partnerships and the gains earned by lasting, real relationships. To everyone who has ever partnered with me and to those who have stood by me as I play long-term games—you are my long-term people, and I thank you.

My father, a mountain man of many talents but few words, taught me the difference between betting and gambling, the value of grit, and the 3 D's: Drive, Determination, and Desire. From winning the 1983 World Championship of Blackjack and teaching me how to place bets to pre-dawn horseback rides in freezing temperatures above timberline, you've shown me that life is a game worth playing well.

My mother, the epitome of compassion, taught me that the world's greatest superpower is helping others. Whether it's being the only one to hold a friend or family member's hand during their battle with cancer or lending an ear to someone who needs to be heard, you've shown me that caring is a gift that enriches both the giver and the receiver.

To the partnership between my parents, a union that has built not only a family but also a business that spans decades—you've modeled the power of partnerships from our small desert town on the border of the Navajo Reservation.

To my son, Atom. You changed my world forever. Atoms are the physical fundamental components of all matter. Although you're still young, I will always thank God for you, my first child, my son—and the life-changing power and perspective your life has bestowed upon me. I vow to be the best possible father, friend, and man to you, forever. My buddy bear, I love you.

To my daughter, Sophia. You are named after the Greek word philosophia—which means the "love of wisdom." From the second I knew you were going to be born, I imagined a world where you'd soak up knowledge and gift me and the world with truth. I promise to always be true to you, cheer for you, and foster your deep-seated curiosity for life. My sweet pea, I love you.

To Isaac Morehouse, my business partner, friend, and chosen older brother, I am blessed to have you in my life. When I think of playing "long-term games with long-term people," I'm motivated to become the best version of myself because of you. To say partnering with you is an honor is an understatement.

To Alex Hernandez, my right hand, confidant, and chosen younger brother, thank you for trusting me to pour knowledge into you. Unknowingly, you would pour right back into me. Because of you, my cup overfloweth.

To every mentor, role model, and partner in my growth, the grace you've shown me has been invaluable. While there are too many to list, I must name a few who changed the course of my life definitively or helped me when I needed it most. Dr. David Bramhall, Dr. Thomas Taylor, Dr. Ron Paul, Jeff Frazee, Alexander McCobin, Mikita Mikado, Serge Barysiuk, the team at HubSpot, Peter Caputa, Kevin Raheja, Matt Cameron, Bobby Napiltonia, David Cancel, Elias Torres, Jill Rowley, Amelia Taylor, Jayme Gonzales, Jay McBain, Asher Matthew, the OG PartnerHackers (you know who you are), our investors in PartnerHacker, my editors Charlie Deist, Shawnie Hamer, designer Taiesha Turner, and to the creator of the word "nearbound," Simon Bouchez—you've each left an indelible mark on my journey. Thank you in particular, Simon, for trusting me with helping take nearbound mainstream.

I stand on the shoulders of giants.

To my team at Reveal (who endure my unconventional style and compulsive, passionate obsessions daily), your tireless efforts in serving our customers and the market are transforming an industry forever, thank you.

To every evangelist of the nearbound movement, every customer, every partner, every member at nearbound.com, and every reader—your support, both big and small, means the world to me. This book truly is for you.

Finally, if my network is my net worth, then I am indeed a fortunate man. My greatest assets, undoubtedly, are my nearbound network and the partnerships that have made my life possible. You've helped me

## ACKNOWLEDGEMENTS

transform what was once an opportunity into a responsibility. A responsibility I take very seriously. This book, and my life's mission—to build a world where everyone can win together—would not be possible without you.

Thank you for your partnership.

If you are reading this, I have one wish: that this book is not merely helpful to your business but transformative in your life. There are ample stories, tactics, strategies, data-backed details, and analyses that will benefit you as a leader in the new world of B2B. But most of all, I share with every ounce of passion I can muster, a first-principle-driven approach that applies well beyond GTM or partnerships.

I will measure *Nearbound and the Rise of the Who Economy's* ultimate success not by the number of copies distributed or Amazon ranking, but instead by the number of times you pick it back up and wrestle with the ideas and practices. I'll leave you with this quote by Jerzy Gregorek, perhaps my favorite quote of all time: "Hard choices, easy life. Easy choices, hard life."

Nearbound is simple but not easy. The changes are simple enough if you start at the fundamentals: the behavior, mindset, and principles a company must adopt to succeed with partnerships. But easy? If it were, everyone would already be doing it.

The ideas in this book will force hard conversations internally and externally. It will force hard choices in your business and in your life. I challenge all who are reading this to "choose hard."

Adapting to this way of thinking requires curiosity, courage, and conviction. And as some of you will come to learn, when you make the hard choices and feel the conviction in your bones, life gets easier after the choices you make get harder.

So, a special thanks to each of you who embarks on this journey with an open mind and the world at your feet.

The business world needs a change: it needs a resistance, it needs a revolution, it needs a movement. And you are that movement.

So get moving.
Stay curious.
Be courageous.
Find your conviction.

— Jared Fuller

# FOREWORD
By Jay McBain

In making the case for nearbound, I like to let the numbers do the talking.

Today, 75% of the $105 trillion world economy is sold through partners. This is across 27 industries and 193 countries. You probably bought your last new car from a dealer, your last TV from a retailer, and your last prescription from a pharmacy. You even bought your last jar of peanut butter from a grocer. Everything happens this way.

But this 75% is more transactional than strategic. It's based on traditional channels such as retailers, dealers, resellers, franchises, agents, and brokers, where partners are primarily intermediaries for distribution rather than influential relationships that can surround the customer journey. That's where the world is shifting. The $5 trillion tech industry follows the same pattern where 73.1% of it flowed through, with, and to partners. Interestingly, for every dollar spent on software and hardware, $2 is spent on services (and growing). In 2023, tech services grew to be larger than telco services for the first time.

Why do I share these numbers? Because a few years back, I declared that we were in the "Decade of the Ecosystem." After the "Decade of Sales" beginning in 1999 and the "Decade of Marketing" in 2009, all data pointed to a once-in-a-generation shift in the global economy—one focused on going to market by influencing the customer with a network of trusted nodes (in a word, *nearbound*).

If you listen to McKinsey, for example, which operates within the boardrooms of Fortune 500 companies, they now report that 82% of CEOs are investing more in partnerships. These aren't just tech partnerships. They encompass leaders in pharmaceuticals, banking, insurance, manufacturing, and automotive. Every company in every industry is essentially mirroring tech companies' approach to ecosystems, and CEOs are now talking about how to leverage nearbound.

Everyone now knows that going at it alone is not an option. Not just because of the billions of dollars in revenue opportunities but because of how the customer wants to buy.

91% of customers place a higher priority on how a product integrates into their lives or workflows over its price, service, and brand reputation, indicating the growing importance of integration-first buying behavior among customers. The story the data is telling is simple: 91% of customers prioritize products that work with the tools and people they're already working with—in other words, the people they trust.

The economics of partnering are changing rapidly. Companies across the spectrum are rethinking their approach to distribution, adjusting to the new realities of customer buying habits and an expanding software stack that must interoperate. New programs and structures are emerging, and companies need to adapt to these changes to stay competitive and maximize their profitability.

A shift this big needs a voice. There are thousands of watering holes in the enterprise and tech channel world where people congregate, learn, and swap ideas. But the transformation from the traditional channel framework to an ecosystem approach requires new ideas, new frameworks, and a new lexicon.

I've been following this transformation for most of my career. I can give you stats to validate every trend and inform every prediction. But humans will lead the Decade of the Ecosystem, and humans need more than data. Humans need narratives. They need stories and mental models that connect data dots into an understandable arc.

Nearbound is the leading framework helping companies leverage the Decade of Ecosystem, and Jared Fuller is the storyteller for this era. In this book, Jared has given a voice to this growing movement—a rallying flag for all those laboring in the fields of partnerships and ecosystems.

But more than that, with this book, nearbound has been turned into an execution plan. It's now an actionable strategy that allows companies across industries to take advantage of the most recent global shift. There is still work to be done—particularly in bringing together the emergent class of partner-focused startups with established enterprise teams and the world of traditional channels. That work begins with ideas and conversations. It ends in a total transformation of business as we know it.

*Nearbound and the Rise of the Who Economy* is a giant leap forward in the conversation. I expect it will only get better with age, as the ideas and predictions in these pages are borne out in the world.

The nearbound movement is gaining momentum, but it's still early. This means those who see the shift, participate in the conversation, and adjust their lives and business strategies, accordingly, will have a first-mover advantage.

## FOREWORD

We have a chance to be a part of the next phase in this decade-defining shift. This book is solidifying the path forward—a path that will make us active participants in the legacy it is helping to create.

*Nearbound and the Rise of the Who Economy* is going to change the way we think about business. I welcome that change.

Jay McBain, Chief Analyst at Canalys
February 2024

# Part 1
## Foundations

*"A driver for the nearbound strategy was the tidal wave of work-from-home in 2020. Suddenly, you only had emails, socials, and vanity connections. Without a trusted source validating the value of your solution, no decision was made. Your connections became the central nervous system of business, and in that moment, the importance of partners was evident.*

*Fast forward a few years and the world has changed. Relationships and advocacy are the predominant ways to acquire and retain business today. That's how we know relationship management is fast becoming an ecosystem-enabling technology. The glue that weaves the ecosystem together, based on equity, transparency, and mutual value for all."*

— Paul Szemerenyi, CEO of Allbound

# CHAPTER 1
# TRUST IS THE NEW DATA

"You idiot, the KGB is here!"

I barely heard the whisper in my ear through the crowd when a dozen colleagues rushed me out the door and threw me into a car. We sped off.

I thought it was a joke.

"What do you mean, the KGB? Like, *Stalin's KGB?*" I yelled at my colleagues-turned-captors.

"Of course Stalin's KGB. Your joke about the President… you can **never** make a joke about him here. We might not have seen you again. They were waiting for you to say something stupid, then BAM—black bag—and you would've been gone."

They weren't laughing.

I was in Minsk, the capital city of Belarus, speaking to a few hundred techies on how to build sales and partnerships when my ill-fated attempt at humor cut short my engagement.

The joke went like this:

> "According to a Harvard study, only 3% of people trust salespeople. Coincidentally, about 3% of the population are also salespeople. I also hear that's about the same as Lukashenko's approval rating."

When I said it, a roar of laughter erupted, followed by pin-drop silence. I had touched a nerve (or two).

It was 2016. I was leading sales and partnerships for PandaDoc. Though both founders immigrated to the States, back then the tech team HQ still called Minsk, Belarus home.

The day after my talk, the C-suite of HubSpot was flying to Minsk to meet our engineering team.

We were in due diligence.

The next day would mark the biggest day of all of our lives.

That was one year almost to the day after my first conversation with HubSpot Chief Strategy Officer, Brad Coffey, who was coming to meet us.

On that first call, I told him:

> "In less than one year, I am going to be your number one partner globally, and you are going to try to buy me."

I made that promise from an apartment that served as our San Francisco office and, for a few months, my temporary bedroom.

The guts!

We were nobody. I was nobody.

Little did I know that in bulldozing my way to fulfilling that promise, I was about to discover a formula for how to partner up and win together—a formula I repeated three consecutive times, helping to mint two unicorns throughout a discovery process that continues to unfold in tandem with the major shifts taking place in the economy.

We'll return to this story later. For now, let's zoom out to understand these shifts that are setting the stage for everything that follows.

From data to trust, from how to who, and from targeting to surrounding.

## Data Was the New Oil

It was exactly one decade prior to the meetings in Minsk that British mathematician and marketing executive Clive Humby boldly proclaimed, "Data is the new oil."

We were at the beginning of a massive change. Cell phones went from luxury to ubiquitous. Razor flip phones and Blackberries were status objects, and SMS supplanted phone calls as our primary method of communication. The world's information was now at our fingertips and in our pockets. Myspace ruled the social zeitgeist where relationships and communities were built.

For the first time, the experience of sharing and discovering online became normal for all of us. Clive Humby was right. After his prophecy, the race for digital value was on. Mass quantities of data were mined, centralized, and monetized.

And the winners reaped massive rewards. Amazon shares traded at around $30 in 2006. In 2022, they traded around $3,000—a 10,000% increase in value. Salesforce shares traded at $6 in 2006. In 2022, $300—a

5,000% increase in value. Those who listened to Humby and invested accordingly made trillions.

Data helped businesses automate, gain efficiencies, and find and target customers.

*Everyone* wanted the digits.

But it is possible to have too much of a good thing. Today, we're awash in data. Customers have "info fatigue." The noise is overwhelming the signal, and we crave authentic human relationships again.

Data may have been the new oil, but data by itself has lost our trust.

We no longer trust data by itself; it's data's *relationship* to us we care about.

Now, trust is the new data.

## A Crisis of Conviction: Why Trust is Increasing in Value

It wasn't just businesses abusing data. Governments were guilty too. Remember the PATRIOT Act? The NSA? Wikileaks and Edward Snowden? Most became so accustomed to hearing about privacy breaches that we became numb—resigned to the fact that details of our intimate lives were being shared between agencies and corporations. But this has come at a steep price in terms of our attitudes towards each other.

Trust is in crisis. Trust in the old institutions—governments, major media outlets, and official experts—has been steadily eroding. The days when the talking heads on the nightly news or the bureaucrats in Washington enjoyed broad public confidence are waning rapidly. Faith in these societal pillars has been replaced by skepticism, even outright disdain.

At the same time, trust in the new tools and tech platforms that were supposed to bring us together has also failed to live up to their promise. Social networks have become hotbeds of outright "misinformation" and, at minimum, deep polarization. Algorithms feed us only what they think we want to see, creating dangerous filter bubbles. The early utopian visions of an open and connected world feel naive, or at least premature, given today's landscape.

And when it comes to individual trust, we are more suspicious of those we don't know than ever. Membership in community organizations is down. Fewer people have close friends they can confide in. Distrustful attitudes are on the rise, especially toward those outside one's immediate circle. We've become a society of strangers eyeing each other warily.

According to a 2019 report by Pew Research Center, social trust and interpersonal trust have been declining in the United States for decades. The report highlights that fewer Americans trust their fellow citizens, and trust in institutions like government and media has also eroded. This decline in social trust leads to increased suspicion and reduced connectedness among people.

This crisis of trust brings both danger and opportunity. The danger is that it fosters a bunker mentality. People may simply tune out entirely and retreat inward. They may shrink their networks and reduce their exposure to the broader world and potential opportunities within it.

But there is opportunity in this crisis as well. This crisis of trust is a needed correction to the excesses of what my team and I call the "Infocalypse"—the world of information overload. The distrust in data brings some welcome discipline to markets and culture. An increasingly virtual world demands the real. The human. The genuine.

It demands a lot out of your company too, but that will help you in the long run. No matter how strong your willpower and company culture, you will always be shaped by the incentive structure you're in.

A world that doesn't trust easily forces you to be better.

Good.

Because trust is now in such short supply, it has become increasingly valuable and prized. There's no commodity rarer or coveted.

Again, trust is the new data.

Perhaps the clearest signal of this new era is how we make purchasing decisions. We seek relevant perspectives and advice from our networks—from real people we trust. Not faceless corporations.

Here's an example we can all relate to:

Sarah Brazier, an Account Executive at Gong, shared a story on LinkedIn about her brother, a Product Manager. Sarah had asked him what kind of sales outreach he responds to.

His answer? Real referrals from people he knows well. Not the fake ones many sellers try to force with vague associations and clumsy conversation openers:

"We both know Jim!"

"Hey, you have a dog, me too!"

"You breathe? Wow, same here!"

Sarah's brother tunes out these ham-handed attempts to manufacture false familiarity. Let's be real, no one appreciates that type of faked rapport. It simply doesn't work in an age where buyers have finely tuned BS detectors.

Even worse are those email subject lines (always written in all lowercase) signaling something urgent that demands your attention, only to reveal another pitch for some service you don't need. If you're still using these tactics as a marketer or salesperson, are they improving or worsening with time?

What we all want is something real—a genuine connection based on shared context and trust. Something relevant coming from someone known. The fact that Sarah is passing this insight along from her brother, someone she trusts, only furthers the point.

This shift is rewriting the rules of customer engagement across the board. Companies clinging to business as usual are losing ground and losing the trust of consumers and partners alike. Why?

According to Ernst & Young, the number one reason companies invest in partnerships and platforms is because of the "proximity to and engagement with customers." For technology leaders, meeting customers where they are and with whom they already trust is how to be closer to the customer and create engagement that matters.

The opportunity lies in recognizing how buyers make decisions in the new economy.

## The Shift from the How to the Who Economy

In the old How Economy, buyers followed a transactional, linear process. They used search engines like Google to identify solutions, compare specs and reviews, and evaluate vendor content to make decisions. Information was king, and buyers identified with products and brands. For companies, it was about getting the right info to people. Whoever had the best content won.

However, today we find ourselves in a new era—the Who Economy. In the Who Economy, buyers take a radically different approach. They turn first to people they know and trust for guidance. Instead of comparing anonymous product reviews, they rely on experts within their networks to provide recommendations based on real-world experience.

Today's buyers ask, "Who do I know that has solved this problem?" Rather than evaluating vendors based on impersonal content, they identify with advocates who act as guides. The best network wins, not simply the best content.

The data bears this out conclusively:

- Americans face up to 10,000 ad impressions per day, tuning out the overwhelming majority (Deloitte)
- 80% of B2B sales leaders say individuals in the buyer's network have the biggest impact on purchase decisions (HubSpot)

- 76% of buyers say integration with existing tech is a top priority, valuing recommendations from current platforms (EY)
- 82% of sales leaders identify referrals as the best leads, highlighting trust (Williams)
- Deals involving trusted partners have 41% higher win rates and close 35% faster (Reveal)

In the old world, major ad platforms and those who gamed them were King. They served as gatekeepers to customers by controlling access to information.

But today, we see viral YouTube influencers like MrBeast disrupting entire industries practically overnight by leveraging trust within their networks to launch new brands. Networks and relationships trump mere information.

MrBeast built trust with his audience. When he launched a candy bar, it became a best seller immediately. Making candy bars isn't the hard part, getting buyers to **trust** you is.

B2B is not immune to this change. The reality is that traditional outbound sales and inbound marketing performance will continue to decline regardless of messaging. It's not just because of automation or generative AI flooding the market. It's deeper. It's how we buy that's changed. Indeed, how we've been selling is now fundamentally misaligned with how buyers make decisions today.

I'll share a personal example. I've started my mornings with a health supplement called Athletic Greens for years now, solely because it was recommended by entrepreneur and biohacker Tim Ferriss—an influencer I trust. I didn't evaluate ingredients or compare alternatives. My trust in the source of the recommendation drove the purchase.

If that's how we purchase in the Who Economy, then how should B2B companies sell and market?

The answer is a realignment to networks of trust, not oceans of data. It's about connecting people to the right people. Data on people isn't what matters, it's the relation of the data to the people. What is the measure of the strength of those relationships? Trust. Enduring companies will build ecosystems of mutually beneficial partnerships and relationships. They will leverage trusted advisors at every stage of the customer journey. They will partner with influencers, integrators, advisors, advocates, and communities. Sales, marketing, success, and product teams must tap into the power of earned trust and advocacy.

In this new era, the market rewards those focused on the who rather than the how.

| HOW ECONOMY | WHO ECONOMY |
| --- | --- |
| Buyers Google to find solutions | Buyers ask those they trust |
| Buyers compare *product specs* | Buyers see *who else is using it* |
| *Information* is key | *Relationship* is key |
| Companies must *be* the source | Companies partner *with* the source |
| The best *content* wins | The best *network* wins |
| Buyer believes in your *product* | Buyer believes their *sphere of trust* |

## The Progression of Eras: From Sales Digitization to Marketing Automation to Partner Ecosystems

We are in the midst of a Partnerships Moment that will mark a new cycle for business—a new era. Companies with enduring aspirations must recognize that what got them here will not get them there.

But before looking forward to how to navigate the dawning era of partner ecosystems, we must look back at the previous three eras of business—each of which emerged from the technologies available at the time.

### Era 1: The Brand Era (1950s-2000s)

Before the age of digitization, companies relied on brand recognition and broadcast marketing to drive sales. This was the Brand Era of business.

In the Brand Era, business-to-business (B2B) companies relied heavily on indirect channels to reach and influence buyers. They worked through networks of resellers, agencies, brokers, and other intermediaries who controlled access and relationships. Direct marketing was costly and ineffective compared to leveraging established partner networks.

In a pre-digital landscape, there was no way to accurately attribute what marketing channels were directly generating sales. Companies would run billboards, radio and television ads, print newspaper advertisements, and send direct mail campaigns. But they could only guess at the ROI for each of these methods.

There was no way to track a buyer's journey back to the initial touchpoint. No cookies to tie ad impressions to website visits. No CRM data to connect leads to closed deals. Marketing was a spray-and-pray endeavor.

So, brand recognition became the key differentiator. Companies invested heavily in identifying their core values and attributes, distilling them into a brand identity. Logos, taglines, and associating brands with trust, quality, and prestige were paramount—all hashed out over three martini lunches in smoky Madison Avenue restaurants.

Distribution and shelf space mattered. Getting products onto store shelves and into consumers' hands was a supply-driven challenge dependent on relationships with retailers and sell-through.

In this era, famous figures like Walt Disney and Sam Walton exemplified the power of branding to create lasting companies. Their cults of personality and creative vision cast a halo over their products and services, imbuing them with trust from the top down. You bought from Walmart because they had the most, best, and most trusted brands.

Innovation largely flowed from internal ideation rather than being customer-led. Sales were driven by brand reach rather than measurable funnels.

This would all change with the coming digital revolution.

The Brand Era created timeless lessons on the power of identity, reputation, trust, and creativity—components that even data-driven companies would need to champion.

But the next two eras were underpinned by one dominant concept: **data.**

## Era 2: The Outbound Era – Sales Digitization (2000s)

The early 2000s saw the rise of the Sales Digitization Era. This period was marked by the emergence of cloud computing, which transformed business and gave birth to the entire industry of Software as a Service (SaaS), as well as a new go-to-market (GTM) strategy.

Entering the Digital World, technology democratized access to data and customers. B2B companies could now analyze, target, and engage buyers directly without relying on middlemen. Data allowed businesses to efficiently identify prospects, reach them over email or phone, and sell directly to the consumer.

B2B was rebuilt around these direct-to-customer capabilities powered by exponentially increasing data. Relationship selling through indirect channels felt unnecessary.

Customer Relations Management (CRM) systems like Salesforce would soon achieve mainstream adoption, becoming the command centers of sales organizations.

The cloud democratized access to data and computational power. Even small startups could leverage the cloud's storage and flexibility to build and scale applications quickly. This enabled rapid experimentation and innovation built on cloud CRM and sales tools.

The cloud completely reshaped how companies could store and analyze data. Enterprise databases were replaced with cloud CRMs. Teams across organizations could now access, process, and measure sales activity to a decimal.

The impact across industries was staggering. Fledgling startups disrupted established giants. Entirely new categories like cloud infrastructure, SaaS, and mobile apps were born. Legacy players scrambled to adapt or faced extinction.

A less discussed but equally important consequence was the digitization of sales processes. For the first time, each stage of the sales cycle—prospecting, pipeline management, forecasting, customer retention—could be meticulously tracked and optimized with data.

This hyper-focus on sales performance data upended GTM strategies. Email outreach and productivity tools made sellers far more efficient at "outbound" sales, targeting customers based on swaths of demographic and firmographic data. Sales teams were rebuilt around efficiency and scale. And, of course, what could be digitized could be automated. At this point, marketing became tightly coupled with the sales funnel.

## Era 3: The Inbound Era - Marketing Automation (2010s)

Starting in the 2010s, the third era arrived faster with the emergence of Marketing Automation. Rather than simply optimizing sales execution, marketing automation focused on systematically generating and qualifying new "inbound" leads. Growth marketing, demand generation, and other marketing practices emerged as their own digital discipline distinct from traditional brand marketing.

Powered by the cloud, companies could directly access customers through digital channels like social platforms, SEO, content, and paid advertising. Sophisticated marketing stacks let them target buyers based on demographics, interests, and behavior.

Technology enabled an unprecedented level of personalization and automation. Email drips, landing pages, and lead scoring were added to the list of growth levers that marketers could pull. Marketing automation platforms made it easy to handle high volumes of inbound leads, score them, and route them to sales. Marketers could generate and qualify net-new opportunities at scale beyond just outbound prospecting.

No longer did B2B teams have to rely on outbound sales prospecting alone to fill the funnel.

This expanding toolbox allowed marketers to take a balanced outbound *and* inbound approach. Rather than just cold calling and emailing, they could now draw prospects in through valuable content and SEO, and nurture them over time. For the first time, inbound became a scalable and measurable driver of the sales funnel right alongside traditional outbound techniques.

Equally as important, this direct access meant startups and digital disruptors were no longer dependent on incumbent "old boys" business networks. In the past, channels and partnerships were requirements to reach customers. Now, technology provided a shortcut.

For the past decade, we've been living in the Marketing Automation Era. A time defined by technology and direct access to a new market of customers. When one growth channel stopped producing ROI, new channels seemed to emerge to fill the void.

Methods and access to the market were innovating so rapidly that legacy indirect channels failed to adapt at the same pace. New technologies empowered a new generation of companies and jobs where they could build, market, sell, deploy, and retain directly.

In the Outbound and Inbound Eras, digitally native B2B SaaS companies had little to no indirect business. Data was the fuel. Automation was the accelerant. Heck, large swaths of B2B companies even have it in their category names! *"Digital Acceleration," "Sales Acceleration," "Revenue Acceleration."*

Their growth playbook was simple: leverage automation and direct digital access to acquire customers efficiently. Technology enabled them to control their own destiny without relying on external third parties. At least that was the theory.

Despite spectacular successes, cracks began to emerge in this model centered around direct customer control. Sure, there were attempts like uniting sales and marketing (outbound and inbound) under the banner of one "revenue" team. But no matter the nobility of the cause or the end reporting structure, it turns out buyers don't factor in vendor's internal political structures in how they purchase.

The reality is, as consumers, we are sick of the "acceleration" and are tired of being controlled or manipulated into making decisions *we clearly own*. As buyers, we are no longer asking, "How do I solve X?" because there are too many answers, too much data, too much noise, and too little to trust.

We've been polluted by information used against us.
Instead, we trust those who work with us.

## The Nearbound Era - The Rise of Networks & Partner Ecosystems (2020s)

Today, we're undergoing a pendulum swing of sorts. What was true in the Brand Era is somehow back, albeit in new forms. There has been a power shift back towards trust: brands, networks—made up of complex overlapping relationships and partnerships—and ecosystems.

Businesses have always leveraged the power of partnerships. But today's digital world demands a reimagined model. And for this, we can look to good ol' Mother Nature for timeless lessons on understanding resilient business ecosystems.

In nature, diverse ecosystems are highly adaptive. Energy flows efficiently to where it's needed most. Waste is recycled to nourish future growth. The system endures disruptions through interdependence.

Perhaps a bit counterintuitive, ecosystems with a greater diversity of species and environment better recover from disturbances and disruptive events.

What happens when we apply that framework to business relationships?

Well, the very companies that spawned the Outbound and Inbound Eras before, like Salesforce and HubSpot, understood that if you want to go fast, go alone, but if you want to go far, go together. They built communities, diversified networks of relationships, and interdependence to establish dominance during the dawn before the Partner Ecosystem Era.

But digitally-native partnerships of this age aren't like physical channel partnerships of the past. Salesforce and HubSpot constructed 21st-century partner models distinct from traditional channels over time.

To understand this distinction between partnerships of the old and new eras, we first have to define some key terms. "Channel" traditionally referred to networks of third parties like resellers, integrators, and distributors that expanded a vendor's reach and physical proximity to the customer. Companies relied on channel partners to take products to market at scale where they were at a disadvantage over previously established routes to the market.

As analyst Jay McBain (formerly of Forrester and now Chief Analyst at Canalys) described it in the foreword, the traditional transactional channel was focused on reselling. These partners specialized in deal registration, order processing, and customer hand-offs. But there's been "a trifurcation," as McBain puts it. The channel world owns the point of transaction, while the emerging partner world seems to own the points of influence and retention.

As Pete Nicholls, Founder of HubDo, recalls from his time at Cisco Systems in the 1990s, vendors like Cisco relied heavily on transactional channel partners to take their products to market at scale. Nicholls helped build Cisco's channel organization which allowed massive growth by leveraging networks of distributors, resellers, and integrators who were focused on sales transactions. At that time, Cisco had around 2,500 partners in the UK alone, all focused on reselling and order processing. This expansive transactional channel was essential for vendors like Cisco to reach customers at scale before the Internet.

In the Nearbound Era, it's not that the transactional channel entirely disappears, it's just divided.

First is the **influencer channel**. Rather than reselling, these partners advocate early in the buyer journey to build brand awareness and preference. They provide recommendations, validation, and sometimes referrals. For example, a marketing agency might recommend certain vendors but not directly sell or fully own the implementation of their products. Gaining the agency's trust to leverage their domain expertise and relationships is the path to generating and closing pipeline.

Second is the **retention channel**. These partners support post-sale customer success, adoption, expansion, and renewal. Think integrations, change management, or managed services partners.

The **transactional channel**, however, is now rare and fading.

In the past, companies expected individual partners to perform all three roles. This is now rarely the case, especially in SaaS, with most customers contracting directly with the vendor. Now, partners play specific roles depending on their strengths.

The lines have blurred. Even the big corporations still left over from the tail-end of the Brand Era—companies like Oracle, Microsoft, SAP, and Intuit—are changing their indirect motions for this new era. Most telling is that over 80% of Microsoft's massive influx of new partners are non-transacting—focused on awareness, advocacy, and retention rather than direct sales.

To McBain, today's channel leaders can no longer take the narrow transactional view. He predicts that millions of 'shadow channels' will emerge around the edges of formal programs not built for channel. What are these programs? They are the partner programs many SaaS companies are iterating on today.

The enduring companies have evolved from dependence on traditional reseller channels. Even HubSpot—which began its entire famed agency program as a siloed, indirect channel—has morphed into an overlay motion on top of the direct sales team. Leaders like HubSpot are investing in ecosystems with diverse partner types that together expand reach across each department.

In maturing ecosystems, some partners specialize in awareness and advocacy early in the buyer journey. Others facilitate activation, retention, or support overall customer growth. But few partners do it all. And even the ones that do don't necessarily do it for every customer, every time. Partnerships, as they are today, are distinct from "channel."

The interplay of partners affecting different parts of the customer journey at different times makes modern ecosystems inherently more robust and adaptive. Information diffuses rapidly through decentralized networks. Value migrates fluidly to wherever it's most needed. The system gains resilience through 'biodiversity' in each B2B ecosystem.

If we take what we've learned and overlay B2B with Mother Nature, we'd come up with a definition of a B2B Ecosystem that looks like this:

> A B2B Ecosystem consists of all networked accounts and contacts linked to the commerce and information they share.
>
> B2B Ecosystems manifest in the form of partnerships (accounts) and relationships (contacts) that either directly or indirectly benefit the end customer (user) of the B2B Ecosystem parent.
>
> Partners are companies with a shared commercial interest. Communities and networks are made up of individuals with shared professional interests and relationships.
>
> The environments in which they interact are defined by markets and often (but not always) segmented by vertical (industry), horizontal (persona), segment (size), and territory (geography).
>
> These components are linked through flywheels of commerce and information.
>
> Like ecological systems, the greater the diversity of a B2B Ecosystem, the greater the resistance and resilience in the face of company, customer, partner, community, market disturbance, competition, or other unforeseen disruptive events.
>
> In B2B Ecosystems, cost and time are conserved.
>
> Information flows through the system like energy—typically from influence to commerce—while trust, like nutrients, is recycled, preserved, and grown.

Thriving B2B ecosystems mirror systems of ecology. The reality is that ecosystems are everywhere. They are at the foundation of all life. And the more diverse and, hence, stable the ecosystem, the more it thrives.

My friend and Lead Strategist & Evangelist for nearbound.com, Jill Rowley, says that the old data-fueled outbound and inbound programs won't vanish overnight, if at all. However, she notes that the winners in the Nearbound Era will complement and supercharge their GTM through the nourishment of trust. This era's B2B leaders are conserving cost and time for their customers while simultaneously and intentionally upcycling trust.

## The New World Hates Friction

As Matt Cameron, CEO of SaaSy Sales Leadership, observes, "Outbound continues to decline in effectiveness due to automation, volume, and defensive tech in inboxes and on phones. Content marketing works to drive inbound, but content is the new spam."

He notes that people have always preferred to take calls from those they know and trust. Buyers rarely consider options that don't come from a referral from within their trusted network.

So, how will business be done in the future?

Cameron answers, "Through trusted communities and referral networks that have not been diluted by inauthentic actors."

What if we could live and work in a world where customers weren't overwhelmed by endless, noisy data and messaging? Where every interaction felt human and relevant.

Where trusted advisors were easy to identify and connect with, and buyers relied on experts within their networks to guide purchasing decisions.

A world where companies leverage partnerships at every step of the customer journey and tap into relationships to expand reach and provide support.

Imagine if sales wasn't just about data and activity, but instead focused on deeply understanding the customer, helping them reach their goals, and surrounding buyers with those they trust. Where B2B models are diverse, resilient, and add value for all participants. A world where trusted information flows freely through nodes in a network.

Where the friction of information is replaced by trusted recommendations. A world where a company's go-to-market actually matches how humans act in the market today.

This world is possible through a strategy called nearbound.

Nearbound is where the company's partnerships and network of relationships are not simply a "channel," nor a partnerships department, but instead a strategy for every department.

Nearbound means overlaying each department with a network of trusted relationships that support how people act in the market, instead of merely trying to get the attention of actors in the market. Nearbound is about tapping into existing connections and relationships *in every department of your company*. It's about strategically partnering throughout the customer lifecycle, a job across every department, and a responsibility for every employee.

As outbound and inbound yield diminishing returns in targeting or attracting buyers, nearbound produces compound interest for established firms and scrappy disruptors alike to surround their buyers with increased efficiency.

Microsoft generates 95% of its revenue with partners. By focusing entirely on a vast ecosystem of advisors, influencers, and advocates, they unlock exponential reach and loyalty. MrBeast similarly leverages trust with his audience to launch new brands overnight. And outbound and inbound leaders like Salesforce and HubSpot have stayed on top of their respective industries by incorporating partnerships into every department, each with thriving ecosystems.

The world's most resilient and adaptive companies make ecosystem-mindedness central to their DNA. Their networks become core competitive assets.

The future is nearbound deals won through influential referrers, frictionless buying journeys, and retention support from trusted sources. The new world hates friction, and the solution is trust.

## Where does Trust Come From? The Promised Land

Nearbound strategies tap into the trust of voices who can help customers get to the places they want to go.

Repeat this mantra after me:

**Trust comes from helping others reach their promised land.**

However, many sellers still operate in the opposite way, not fully understanding buyers' desired outcomes.

Let's contrast how people buy today with the traditional sales approaches. Nowadays, we seek out and listen to people who have already been where we want to go—who have done the thing we're trying to do. Their journey inspires trust because of their likeness to who we are and/or the vision of who we want to be. This makes us eager to let them help guide our purchases.

For example, I wanted to take up long-distance running. In my journey to learning about ultra-marathons, I found myself geeking out on the stories of runners who achieve greatness, and I'd follow them. Zach Bitter, for example, blew my mind when he broke the 100-mile speed record. Not only could he run far, but fast. Shockingly, he would never get knee injuries even during his most intensive training schedules. I learned the way Zach runs is a mid-foot strike, utilizing the natural movement of toes, knees, and hips that require a different shoe style than the forced heel strike imposed by Nike.

Zach runs on Altra. Altra boasts a wide toe-box, zero-drop heel, and light sole. Guess who else runs on Altra now? Me. Why do I buy them? Zach Bitter. He's been to the promised land. I trust him. I've followed his story. And most purchases today follow the same pattern.

When we're looking to buy a car, are we going to talk to people who own the models we've been eyeing, or will we trust a sales rep who is desperate to hit quota for the week with the inventory on hand?

And when was the last time you used a review site? Nowadays, everything from restaurants to hotels to attractions has the standard 4.7 stars. In a world of data, all gameable games get gamed. Reviews are no exception.

We don't trust companies who offer the promised land.

Instead, we trust the people who *have actually been to our promised land*.

We identify with those already living the reality we seek—whether that's running a marathon in under four hours for the first time, or thriving as a Chief Information Officer (CIO) of a global enterprise.

We trust those who put their money where their mouth is. They have experience investing in and being rewarded for doing something we have not done.

The sales rep may know their product specs cold, but can they personally relate to my situation? Have they lived the experience I'm trying to create by using this product? More likely than not, there's a massive disconnect.

Think of a sales call with a CIO. As the rep, we may pitch our platform's technical capabilities and ROI models, but have we actually been a CIO managing complex infrastructure at scale before?

Let's be real, if we're selling to a CIO, it's not likely we've actually **been** a CIO. No wonder the CIO will be skeptical of a seller's guidance. Sellers aren't helping them reach their promised land from a place of shared experience.

Too much of sales still fixates on volume-driven metrics versus truly understanding customers' journeys. The focus is on numbers, calls, pipelines, demos, product pitches, objections, and discounts—chasing the close. These are all seller-centric motions.

Nowhere on that list is *doing the actual job your customers want you to do*—immersing yourself in their world to grasp their real-life challenges, goals, and motivations.

Without living your customers' journey first, how can you expect to earn their trust to guide them to where they want to go?

Let me state this emphatically: You can't because **YOU *wouldn't even trust YOURSELF.***

It's true.

Think of influencers we follow on social media. We don't book travel based on unknown agents' promises. We plan trips inspired by accounts we follow, cultivating the lifestyles and experiences we crave. They've literally been to that place, went to that restaurant, took that tour, and slept in that hotel.

People don't want empty promises of a dream life, experience, or product. They want help achieving their goals from others who understand the journey intimately, and tacitly.

Nearbound companies realize sales is no longer about selling. It's about forging relationships based on helping customers become who they aspire to be. It's about surrounding the customer with those who have been there to help them get there.

Yes, trust comes from helping others reach their promised land. But we only trust those who've been to the places we want to go.

If you haven't been where you buyer wants to go, you'd better partner with someone who has.

## Reap The Benefits

For companies stuck in previous eras, a nearbound approach may seem risky. Throughout this book, I hope to eradicate this fear. Not only are the rewards of nearbound motions immense, but they can be easily overlaid to every department across every employee. Here are just a few of the benefits you can expect with nearbound:

- By tapping into relationships of trust, you spend less on cold prospecting while closing deals faster.
- Customers stay loyal longer through expanded advocacy and reduced churn.

- Diverse participants make your ecosystem more innovative and resilient to disruption.
- Costs decline as influencers increasingly endorse your brand to motivated buyers.
- The networked database of partners provides new data to complete insights across the customer lifecycle.
- Most importantly, gains compound across all areas of business. Revenue, efficiency, and performance rise in unison.

This is only a glimpse of the benefits enabled by prioritizing trust-based relationships and ecosystems. The high-value outcomes multiply every year as your partnerships earn compound interest.

## Strategy is Choice and Not All Choices Are Equal

Throughout this book, we're going to take a serious look at leaders, companies, and industries far and wide being changed forever by nearbound strategies. But I don't speak about this topic so passionately and inquire so deeply based on mere curiosity. I speak based on conviction. I haven't always won in business, but when I have, nearbound is how I've done it.

I've learned through first-hand experience and from great category creators that the most misunderstood word in startups is "strategy." Strategy is choice. Period. And not all choices are equal.

Getting back to my HubSpot and PandaDoc Belarus story, I figured out how to go from nothing to the number one partner of the most important company in our ecosystem. I made the right choice, even if, at the time, I didn't know exactly why I was right. The right strategy was simply the right choices.

I uncovered an art and a formula. How to partner up and win together. I detailed my recipe fully in a chapter of *The PartnerHacker Handbook* called, "Strategic Alliances: PartnerUp and Play to Win." I bring it up here to illustrate who I am and to tell you this bet works—not just from stories I've heard, but stories I've lived.

The proof is real.

When HubSpot CRM launched, it was in the most competitive SaaS industry: SMB CRM. PandaDoc was an e-sign and proposal tool. At the time, HubSpot was already a juggernaut public Martech SaaS company, but it was so early on its platform journey that HubSpot CRM didn't yet have APIs.

But I knew they'd win CRM and, for PandaDoc, that meant we **had** to be their number one.

The year we went after them, we found out that HubSpot CRM's most important metric was activating trial signups. We also uncovered that the most important metric for taking a signup to a paying customer was moving a deal to closed won. Moving a deal to closed won meant a 700% increase in the likelihood a customer would pay for HubSpot.

And that's exactly what PandaDoc did. It helped people close deals.

The full story is pretty wild (you can hear it on the Nearbound Podcast Episode #001 if you are so inclined) but the short version is this:

- PandaDoc hacked a Chrome extension which allowed it to send documents from HubSpot even without access to their APIs. This was nearbound product innovation in action.
- We got a few dozen joint customers to use it and even sent a few customers to HubSpot to try it out.
- We discovered that PandaDoc cleared the friction for closing a deal and moving their first opportunity to closed won at a faster rate and with higher predictability **than any other single HubSpot partner**.

So, we both sped up.

- We did nearbound marketing across events, emails, social, and even partner ads.
- We did nearbound sales across our account executives and their account teams.
- We did nearbound success by having our CSMs connect every single joint customer's integration.
- We did nearbound product innovation by being one of the first-ever partners to build on HubSpot CRM's first-ever published API.

Less than one year later, PandaDoc was HubSpot's number one partner-built CRM integration.

We were so successful that we even convinced HubSpot to kill their own internal e-sign project and instead cut their first-ever venture check. Our nearbound motions worked so well that HubSpot Ventures was formed, and PandaDoc was the first ever check HubSpot cut to invest in another SaaS company.

I could go on with another dozen stories about big nearbound choices with Marketo and Drift…

How we took over Adobe Summit and the main stage keynote after a fabled meeting with Jill Rowley and Bobby Napiltonia...

How we became Adobe's Partner of the Year out of 1,700 other partners...

Or how we won over 1,000 accounts from nearbound choices.

I've used partnerships and relationships to establish strategic alliances with three different sumos and to advise dozens of other startups. I've helped mint two unicorns and led the sales, marketing, success, and product teams to surround the customers where they live, not merely where we want them to be.

And since PandaDoc and Drift, I've arguably spoken to more partner leaders and written more about B2B technology partnerships than perhaps anyone on the planet. The nearbound.com media network (formerly PartnerHacker), is the largest library of partner and GTM-related content anywhere.

What I've come to learn both through my experiences and thousands of conversations and pieces of content is this: **nearbound is aligned to the modern buyer's journey, and that makes it the best lever for B2B leaders.**

The opportunity is massive for visionary leaders who embrace partnerships at the core of their overall business strategy. This book reveals how to transform your organization into a pioneer of the Nearbound Era.

I will show you how to build partnership strategies into the DNA of every department—from product to marketing to sales to customer success to operations. Nearbound is the antithesis to the plague of siloed partnership teams. Nearbound is the clarion call for a company-wide mindset and manuscript for each department's alignment.

You will learn to harness relationships already hidden in your network and become a guiding light for others still cursing at the heaps of data that have left everyone busier than ever with no more efficiency to show for it. These lessons are not reserved for the converted nor for the so-called experts. This book and its lessons are accessible to and implementable by everyone.

In the coming chapters, we'll unpack fulfilling your and your company's potential in the Nearbound Era. No more partnerships as a walled-off channel or singular department, but instead, partnerships as a strategy for every department.

Not all choices for marketing, sales, customer success, product, partnerships, social networks, and operations are equal—nor are they all easy. Layering nearbound onto every department is fairly basic. It's what David Cancel, the CEO of Drift, would call "simple, not easy."

But absent a new way of looking at business and markets, this task can feel both complex **and** difficult.

It doesn't have to be. From first principles built on solid foundations to success stories across every sector, the chapters ahead will show how nearbound makes the world go round.

But before we unpack how you can apply it, let's define it.

What is *nearbound*, anyway?

CHAPTER 2

# NEARBOUND DEFINED

*Outbound → Inbound → Nearbound*

At its core, nearbound is the next evolution of go-to-market motions that builds upon the mass adoption of outbound and inbound models.

In the past, outbound sales motions were primarily associated with the sales department, while inbound was connected to marketing. However, nearbound is not solely defined by the partnerships department. Instead, nearbound is an integrated motion and strategy that encompasses every department.

AppBind CEO Sunir Shah likes to say, "The only reason partnerships should exist is because customers want them."

It is important to recognize that nearbound has emerged in response to customer preferences and actions. It is not a speculative exercise. It's an acknowledgment of reality. Buyer behavior has evolved, and go-to-market strategies should adapt to and embrace this change instead of resisting it.

To understand what nearbound is, let's break it down using this formula:

- Nearbound in a word
- Nearbound in a sentence
- Nearbound in a paragraph
- Nearbound in a page
- Nearbound in a chapter (this one!)
- Nearbound in a book (the rest of this book)

## Nearbound in a Word

Surround.

## Nearbound in a Sentence

A business strategy that connects to buyers with and through the network of partnerships and relationships that surround them.

## Nearbound in a Paragraph

Nearbound is a business strategy that connects to buyers through the network of partnerships and relationships that surround them. As a B2B Go-To-Market (GTM) motion, nearbound can be overlayed to outbound and inbound strategies. The difference lies in the foundation: outbound targets the customer, inbound attracts the customer, and nearbound surrounds the customer. With the advent of the networked database, "2nd party data" or "nearbound data" provides the most valuable signal to surround your top accounts, customers, influencers, and partners. In a world where trust is the new data, companies that prioritize identifying, collaborating, and executing nearbound plays with influential partners have the advantage.

## Nearbound in a Page

Nearbound transforms linear funnels into multifaceted flywheels, leveraging existing customers as sources of new leads and current partners as hubs for intelligence, influence, or introductions to your top accounts. To achieve this, nearbound shifts partnerships from being limited to a specific department to becoming a strategy implemented across the entire organization.

The nearbound approach aligns your overarching operating model with a broader ecosystem, beyond just internal operational metrics. This strategy is based on the principle of network effects, where the value of your services or products increases as they become integrated and utilized within a larger system. By embracing this concept, your company transitions from a peripheral role to becoming a central node within this interconnected network. In this new paradigm, relying solely on your own data is no longer sufficient. Instead, you leverage your networked database to drive new choices, programs, processes, and technology that enable nearbound initiatives throughout every department.

While outbound focuses on targeting customers and inbound strategies aim to attract them, nearbound *surrounds* customers with trust at every stage of their journey.

But where does this trust come from? It starts with understanding customers' aspirations and helping guide them to their promised land. We place faith in those who have already been where we want to go. This means leveraging your partners' authority and influence to inject trust—from enabling an all-new ability to providing simple credibility—across the entire customer journey.

Your own sales or marketing teams may be skilled, but chances are they haven't personally solved your customers' specific problems before. They've never been to the promised land. If you run a technology company, your team markets and sells access, not outcomes. Look no further than their obvious compensation metrics to confirm this. In the Nearbound Era, you may have a perfect pitch, but buyers aren't buying it if it's coming from a perfect stranger. You require connection to their network and relationships, and context of information filtered by someone they trust.

As HubSpot CEO Yamini Rangan outlined in her essay "The Age of the Connected Customer," buyers are bombarded at every turn. People are drained from endless notifications across our devices and accounts—they filter because they have no other choice.

This disconnect is apparent in the data regarding how buyers engage today, particularly since the pandemic-driven surge in remote collaboration tools. Companies have adopted numerous separate tools and workflows. Consequently, a disconnect has emerged between us and our customers. We now appear more like strangers to them. They lack the necessary context and feel isolated.

According to *Business Insider*, by the end of 2020, 65% of Google searches did not result in a click. Additionally, HubSpot reports that blog readership declined and response rates to sales outreach dropped by 40% compared to pre-pandemic levels.

When Yamini discusses the age of the connected customer, characterized by the importance of relationship context rather than solely data management, she could just as easily be referring to the Nearbound Era described in the previous chapter.

Before adopting another tool or integration, connected customers are asking themselves:

- Will this integration simplify my life enough to justify the additional setup time?
- Will it align with my current workflows, software, and routines, or will it introduce another potential point of failure?

- Is it worth managing another password, risking another data breach, or adding another service provider or consultant to handle it?
- Will it pass a straightforward cost/benefit analysis in a time of budget cuts?

"You need more than data, you need context," Rangan says. She adds that connection is more important than information and that community is more important than contacts.

Coming from anyone other than the CEO of HubSpot, this might just sound like a platitude. However, since taking over the company in 2021, Rangan has done an excellent job steering HubSpot from the Marketing Automation Era of the 2010s into the Nearbound Era. The way to win is changing because the way we buy is changing forever. Addressing this shift in how we think and what we need as buyers is not an intractable or shapeless problem. On the contrary, some first principles are driving the undercurrent of nearbound.

## Nearbound in a Chapter: Building Up from First Principles

Warren Buffett surprised his followers when he stated that Berkshire Hathaway's remarkable success in creating value for over 50 years can be attributed to only 12 crucial strategic decisions. This means that, on average, a significant decision was made every four to five years, resulting in an astonishing return of over 3,400,000% for their shareholders.

Let's take a moment to contemplate this. Buffett's point is that extraordinary results do not arise from numerous small tactical choices. Instead, they stem from a select few, exceptional, high-impact decisions that are guided by first principles.

Berkshire Hathaway's decision-making process is a prime example of Annie Duke's *Thinking in Bets*, which is a response to a world that operates on probabilities. When executed correctly, this approach yields significant returns that are not merely exceptions, but rather the standard. It is a fundamental principle that leads to making the right choices.

Investors who attempt to mimic Buffett's every move may be disappointed when they fail to achieve similar results in their portfolios. By the time you try to replicate Berkshire Hathaway's strategy, the opportunity may have already passed. Those who acted early and remained committed to their principles will have already reaped the rewards.

Progress, growth, and change naturally stem from first principles.

Another well-known example is the "Pareto Principle," which states that in a natural state, 80% of output comes from 20% of input. In the current investment climate, the stakes are even higher: 99% of supernormal returns may come from just 1% of decisions. Peter Thiel popularized a related concept as his first rule of contrarian investing, based on a mathematical "power law" distribution. This distribution predicts that investors in a fund will achieve a 10x return from a single "unicorn" that outperforms the rest of the portfolio by 100x. (We'll return to what this principle means for you individually at the end of this book.)

What was considered contrarian thinking 10 years ago has now become conventional wisdom. Companies have embraced this mindset and are striving to lead their respective markets by establishing a lasting and effective model that recognizes the potential of these high-risk, high-reward bets, rather than opposing them.

But when we look at traditional inbound and outbound models, we see textbook-perfect competition, not bets. Companies are cycling through dozens of tactics—making hundreds of decisions that turn out to be inconsequential.

The result? We know it. Buyers are not responding to the same old techniques that are being recycled in a new form. They are experiencing message saturation and information overload at a profound level. Yet many companies continue to invest mental energy in these tactics, becoming exhausted by their failure to acknowledge the underlying shifts taking place.

Business leaders navigating the current landscape face a crucial decision that will determine our success in the coming decade. Should we commit to probabilistic thinking, take calculated risks, and make strategic choices? Or should we hold onto outdated go-to-market practices?

In this era, trust trumps data. Relationships supersede messaging. And network effects compound growth in ways that linear funnels cannot.

The organizations poised to win have embedded partnership ecosystems and nearbound thinking into their DNA. They have evolved within the partnership ecosystem to surround customers with credible influencers rather than simply targeting them with clickbait or phony sales pitches.

Make no mistake, we stand at the precipice of the Nearbound Era. You don't need to make 100 choices; you just need to make *this one*:

Partner up or perish. Evolve or die.

# Why Nearbound, Why Now

## HubSpot & Peter Caputa: The Power of Strategic Partnerships

Although HubSpot is best known as a pioneer of inbound marketing software, it is my favorite example of a company that recognized the strategic power of partnerships early on. Over time, they embedded a nearbound strategy into their DNA, even if they didn't call it by that name at the time.

I refer to them a lot for good reason. As a business, HubSpot performs. It is one of the most consistently performing companies on the Nasdaq. During an interview with Dharmesh Shah on *The 20 Minute VC*, host Harry Stebbings highlighted that HubSpot has never missed earnings since going public. Their approach paid off, but where did it start?

Peter Caputa, one of the initial five Account Executives at HubSpot and later the CEO of Databox, played a significant role in instilling this mindset at the company. Under Pete's leadership, the agency partner program grew from $0 to $100M in ARR, bringing about a transformative impact not only for HubSpot but also for the entire marketing services industry. (It's worth noting the trend of industry-defining partner leaders later becoming CEOs.)

Most businesses viewed partnerships through the narrow lens of how they benefited end customers. But Pete understood the importance of developing partners holistically.

"For me, everything about working with these agencies was about helping them build a better business," Pete explained during a podcast interview I did with him a few years back.

Having previously owned an agency himself, Pete grasped this principle at a fundamental level. He had lived the challenges agencies faced. He had been to their promised land. He knew how to craft a program focused on empowering partners to solve their internal business challenges, not just selling them products.

There was initial resistance within HubSpot regarding heavy investment in agency partners, but the results soon spoke for themselves. Pete helped agencies evolve to more sustainable business models built on recurring revenue. HubSpot provided them with the tools and content they needed to make this transition. Pete built a program and an entire business unit around assisting agencies in changing how they billed their clients, the products and services they offered, and even the decisions on who they served—narrowing down their focus to expand their reach.

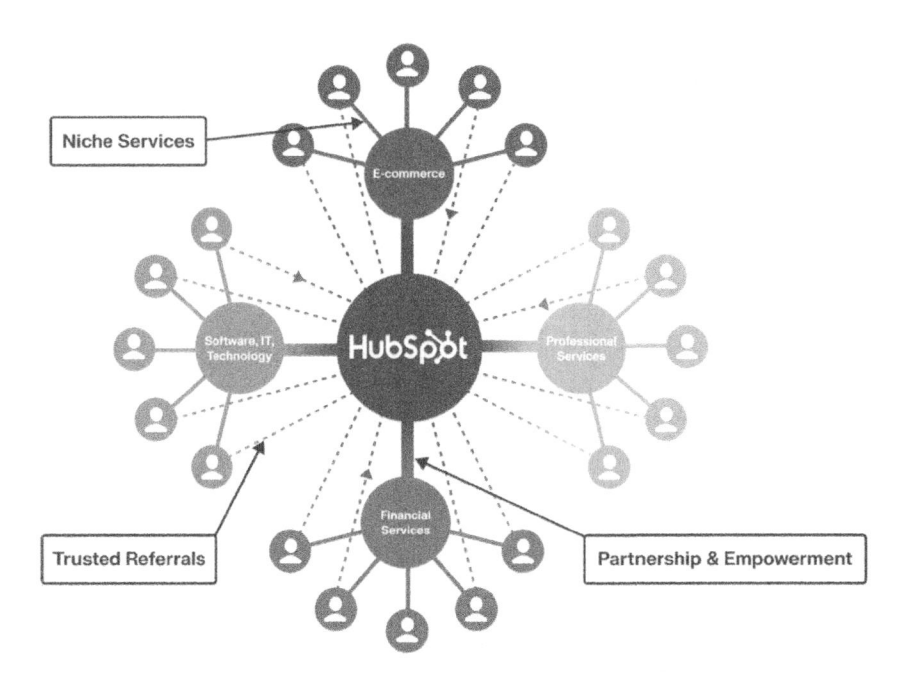

*HubSpot's partner strategy*

By promoting greater specialization, his programs transformed generalist agencies into established niches. For instance, an agency that served healthcare clients was encouraged to position itself as a healthcare marketing specialist instead of another "yes, we can" do-it-all agency. This shift led to increased client retention and referrals as clients began to see agencies not as interchangeable commodities, but as networks of specialized experts. Proximity also became an advantage, as agencies were more likely to win business from new prospects referred by existing clients within their immediate network.

Over time, Pete's fingerprints helped HubSpot to make partners the center of everything—events, content, and community building—related to the Inbound movement. He knew that their success would ultimately drive HubSpot's success. This set a network effect in motion: a flywheel. As agencies thrived in their niche, their clients would refer new prospects from within the same industry. HubSpot would gain these new customers through trusted referrals within close-knit professional networks.

# NEARBOUND DEFINED

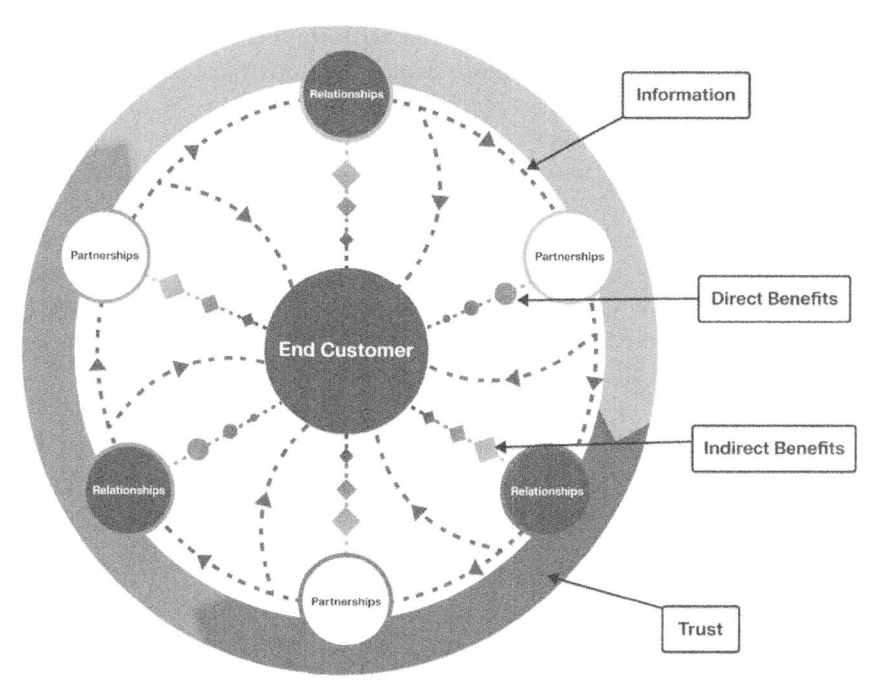

*The partnerships flywheel*

This flywheel transformed HubSpot into a public multi-billion-dollar leader in the marketing industry. In the past, HubSpot was considered a lesser player in marketing automation compared to Eloqua, Pardot, Marketo, and Act-On. But only one of these companies achieved a successful IPO: HubSpot. Part of its endurance can be attributed to its evolution in partnerships. It has transitioned from siloed departments, teams, and business units to more cross-functional programs. This integrated model reflects the ethos of nearbound more effectively than anything that came before.

Mark Roberge, the original sales leader and famed CRO of HubSpot, Harvard lecturer, author of the bestselling book *The Sales Acceleration Formula*, and founder of Stage 2 Capital, fondly reflects on the interesting emergence and eventual scale of the agency business Pete started. However, in our conversations, he has also highlighted the challenges created over time by having "direct" and "indirect" teams operating as separate entities, despite both teams growing rapidly and independently from the success of inbound.

Caputa also felt this pain. "Channel conflict" caused more struggle over time than it was worth. But the reason for its existence in the first place was because the direct SaaS seller couldn't even come close to accomplishing what Pete's team could with the agency funnel. Neither Pete nor Mark takes credit for the eventual solution at scale, but both were crucial to the shift. Since the Caputa–Roberge days, HubSpot has transitioned from a channel business unit and direct sales team to an integrated revenue approach. Caputa called this an "overlay model," and my friend Jill Rowley calls it an "infused model."

Whatever you call it, here's the deal: these previously isolated teams no longer measure separately, work separately, or receive compensation separately. They now work together. The combined unit economics drive the business forward—they're not wasting time or energy fighting over credit. And HubSpot's ecosystem and flywheel keep on spinning. What started as a "channel partner" success story now feels a lot more like the modern inbound story in many more ways than HubSpot's agency program.

After achieving a massive impact with HubSpot's agency partnerships, witnessing the IPO, and assisting in launching CRM, Pete went on to apply similar nearbound principles to his next venture, Databox—a reporting dashboard tool tightly integrated with HubSpot. Pete chose to put his energy into Databox specifically because it presented inherent network effect advantages. As a business intelligence and visualization tool, its value grew exponentially based on the breadth of data sources it could connect to. More integrations equaled more partnerships, and more partnerships equaled more delighted customers.

Everything from their content strategy to product roadmap focused on tight ecosystem alignment and surrounding their customers with what they already used. Instead of generic outreach, Pete's team interviewed and highlighted hundreds of existing partners of their integrations—and you bet he tapped into HubSpot agencies. The Databox content strategy made the users and partners famous, and in turn, Databox learned how they could better serve their needs with their product and feedback on their marketing. This produced a sustainable marketing engine attracting adjacent partners into Databox's orbit and new sign-ups from those partners.

The advantages of this strategy have compounded over time. Databox has grown from a fledgling startup to one of HubSpot's most successful integration partners and the number one partner for built-in integration out of thousands. Pete's nearbound mindset (more on this in the closing chapter) paved the way for growth. Today, Databox boasts tens of thousands of customers and has a profitable and sustainable business with hundreds of employees. It is a true nearbound success story. And the best part? Where is Pete's partnerships department? Well, it doesn't really exist. Everyone works this way at Databox. And guess who loves Pete's model the most? His customers and partners.

The playbook Pete established at both HubSpot and Databox exemplifies how pioneering companies embed ecosystems into their DNA across marketing, sales, success, and product teams. They shape strategies around trust-based relationships instead of transactions. These motions create a gravitational force that attracts partners and customers, bringing them into closer proximity to each other and to the software company orchestrating the ecosystem. This proximity generates throughput in the form of compounding gains. This phenomenon is commonly referred to as *network effects*.

While I will return to the specific strategies Pete employed and share more about the HubSpot story repeatedly in future chapters, it is important to first understand a foundation of nearbound—network effects—to fully comprehend why nearbound makes the B2B world go round.

## Network Effects Explained

Although the term "network effects" has become more popular, even those who use it often fail to understand their immense power. Network effects often dwarf all other factors in determining success or failure. Choices, remember?

Network effects and nearbound are closely related concepts. In many ways, nearbound is the ideal GTM strategy for a world where network effects dominate. Once you grasp the meaning and functioning of network effects, you realize the importance of engaging and partnering with the nodes connected to your target audience, rather than relying on inbound and outbound approaches to reach buyers directly.

According to James Currier, a five-time founder and Founding Partner at NFX (with angel investments in Doordash, Lyft, and Patreon, among others), network effects are the most valuable property of a business. They are the one thing shared in common by nearly every major category leader in every industry.

Over the course of a three-year study, NFX concluded that "network effects are responsible for 70% of the value created since the Internet became a thing in 1994 [...and] are the #1 way to create defensibility."

They shared this finding in their *Network Effects Manual: 16 Network Effects (And Counting)*—required reading for anyone interested in the topic.

Currier implores founders to study and master network effects because, "For founders looking to build truly impactful companies, few areas of expertise are more valuable."

How valuable? *70% of the entire Internet valuable.*

Currier's work on the value and application of network effects is compelling. And when you look around, the stories of network effects are everywhere. Even the most disruptive companies in the world partner with their legacy competitors to double down on the value of network effects.

Elon Musk sent shockwaves through the auto industry in 2023 by announcing a game-changing partnership. Tesla would open its proprietary network of over 15,000 supercharging stations to other electric vehicle models, including ostensible competitors like Ford and GM.

Ford or GM *could* develop a better electric car than Tesla on many dimensions. But even the greatest vehicle is useless without ample places to conveniently and rapidly recharge while on the road. And Tesla's multi-year head start has given it a lead in charging availability.

Catching up to Tesla's supercharger network would come at a cost too high and a timeframe too slow for other automakers. Consumers may wait for themselves, but they won't wait for the industry when an existing product and network serve them. Failing to provide adequate charging access to their customers would cripple GM and Ford's sales as they pivot to electric. So, Musk presented them with a third option: join the existing network, make it denser, and collaborate to accelerate EV adoption overall.

It's no surprise that Ford and GM opted to partner rather than compete. No brainer for them, but how so for Tesla? This collaboration reveals Musk's deep grasp of network effects. Tesla's edge doesn't lie solely in its vehicles, but rather in its vast and rapidly-expanding charging infrastructure. The establishment of a supercharging station network has fortified an almost insurmountable competitive barrier. Understanding this concept of defensibility is crucial to grasping the substantial influence of network effects. With each addition to Tesla's expansive charging network, the overall utility escalates, enhancing the value of Tesla vehicles for consumers. This is because every new user or, in Tesla's case, every new charging station, augments the product's value for all participants. Tesla's extensive network of over 15,000 stations makes it almost impossible for any competitor to duplicate this utility for consumers. The network effect, thus, not only amplifies the usefulness of Tesla vehicles but also cements its market stronghold.

Such is the essence of network effects: the value of a network experiences compound growth as new nodes—here, charging stations—are integrated. This exponential advantage underlines why network effects have become the foremost source of defensibility in the digital era.

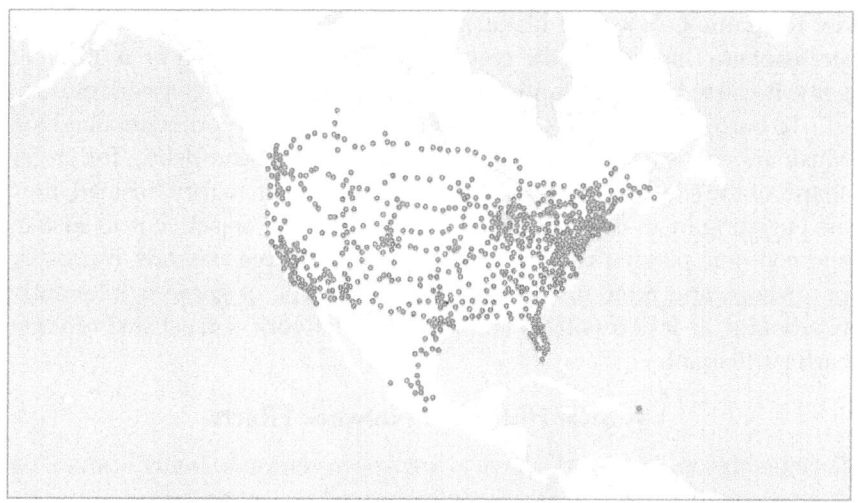

*Tesla Supercharger network, Tesla Digital Assets*

Tesla is playing the long game here. Today, their network is powered by a combination of energy sources. Tomorrow, it will rely on Tesla solar panels and large-scale battery storage, creating a self-sustaining flywheel propelled by this partnership. Elon Musk envisions a distributed network of solar panels and energy generation to support an entirely electric automobile fleet by 2050. That's thinking in bets **and** thinking in network effects. First principles squared.

Most recognize Musk as the greatest entrepreneur of this generation. His intuition and back-of-the-envelope approach to fundamental science have guided him to what could be described as a nearbound go-to-market strategy. It has valuable and defensible network effects acting as a flywheel, transforming what seems like a simple charging station into a global EV platform from which everyone can benefit.

Everyone? Indeed, it's bigger than just Detroit vs. Silicon Valley. Hilton, for example, announced a partnership with Tesla only months later to place 20,000 chargers across 2,000 properties throughout North America. So you have to ask the question: without the support of Ford & GM in the Tesla Supercharger Network, does the Hilton & Tesla partnership ever happen? You don't have to be a rocket scientist or plead your case to the attribution gods, you know the answer. Tesla knew the answer. Musk knew the answer. Compound interest.

Can you imagine Musk worrying about who gets credit for Ford or GM's involvement in the Hilton deal when it comes to Tesla? That's hilarious. Or criticizing SpaceX's calculations for their disruptive Starlink constellation and attributing the T-Mobile partnership to new subscriber touchpoints? It's comical. But that's not the game Musk is playing, and it's not the game he's asking his team to play. He's operating in a different stratosphere (literally, in the case of SpaceX) and focusing on a different game because he understands the power of 21st-century network effects.

To borrow from philosopher James P. Carse, entrepreneurs like Elon Musk are choosing to opt out of the *finite* game of competing for larger shares of the same pie in pursuit of a static notion of victory. Instead, they are engaging in an *infinite* game—one in which the objective is to sustain and continue playing the game. In this game, the pie expands, humanity progresses, and relationships multiply. This type of game is inherently nearbound, as it necessitates and implies a network of trust surrounding each participant.

## A Brief History of Network Effects

Partnerships and networks have always been central to being human. As Aristotle said, humans are social animals. And as we progress as a species, we also progress towards an increasingly interconnected world. Economists David Ricardo and Adam Smith revealed the power of collaboration and the invisible hand in the generation of surplus when two parties specialize in their comparative advantage. We now have the opportunity to make this invisible hand visible and unlock even greater value from mutually beneficial exchange.

Extending this logic to the realm of multiple buyers and sellers, we begin to see the emergence of networks of trade—all interconnected and even interdependent in many cases.

Roads and the *lingua franca* (a bridge language between two non-native speakers) are both examples of network effects that have facilitated the global marketplace we find ourselves in. In the past, routes to market were literal roads. However, the shifting technology landscape—coupled with the crisis of trust—is multiplying the permutations and the importance of network effects. The gravity, proximity, and throughput of these interconnected roads and nodes start to matter at an increasing rate.

Over a century ago, AT&T's President, Theodore Vail observed how an inferior product can dominate with sufficient network scale. He noticed how AT&T's telephone network became nearly impossible to compete with once they amassed more customers in a locale. In his NFX Manual of Network Effects, James Currier uses this as a prime illustration of the immense power of network effects in driving growth and creating defensible positions in the market. By understanding and leveraging the dynamics of networks, companies can tap into the compounding benefits of proximity, gravity, and throughput to amplify their impact and reach. This is the essence of nearbound thinking, where partnerships and ecosystems become the foundation for sustainable growth and success.

This direct network effect meant the core value lay not in the phone itself, but in its connections. As Vail stated, "A telephone—without a connection at the other end of the line—is one of the most useless things in the world."

AT&T's network density created gravity that pulled in users, carved proximity to new nodes, and generated new levels of throughput. Vail's insight was ahead of its time.

It took until the 1970s before the network effect concept became more formally defined and modeled. In 1976, Robert Metcalfe articulated what became known as Metcalfe's Law. It states that the total value of a network grows proportional to the number of users squared.

So, for example, a network with 10 users would provide roughly 100 times more value than a network with 1 user ($10^2 = 100$). And a network of 100 users provides 10,000 times more value than a network of one user ($100^2 = 10,000$).

Metcalfe's Law mathematically framed the direct network effect AT&T exhibited with its telephone network. However, some later thinkers argued it actually underestimated the potential value.

In the 1990s, David Reed postulated that network value grows exponentially faster than the square of users. This is because networks contain sub-networks and local groupings that multiply value.

Think of a high school and its students. Students benefit not only from the overall school network but also from sub-networks like the baseball or volleyball teams that compete with other schools ("Go Panthers!"). If the school's network is larger, there are more opportunities for high-performing sub-networks. Although this example helps to illustrate the concept of sub-networks, it does not effectively convey Reed's point about velocity.

Reed believed that the total value scales exponentially at $2^N$, where N is the number of network users. Reed's Law captures how local clusters and sub-communities within large networks can boost overall utility and effectiveness, thereby attracting more users. In this sense, while Metcalfe's Law helps model direct network scaling, Reed's Law incorporates real human behavior and relationships. Most large networks are not equally distributed—they contain pockets of high density and affinity. Some schools have the best wrestling team in the state, while others come last. In other words, not all networks are equal. Schools lack proximity to other networks and throughput for growth. The physical world may map to Metcalfe, but the digital world is run by Reed.

Digital network experts uncover and architect social mechanisms that strengthen sub-network proximity, gravitational pull, and throughput.

We saw early signs of sophisticated network effect strategies in the previous eras of the digital age (70% of the value of the internet, remember?). For example, unicorns like PayPal, Facebook, Uber, and YouTube emphasized rapid user acquisition in their go-to-market models, incentivizing referrals to tap into both virality and network effects (Currier's work at NFX makes a clear case for how and why virality and network effects, while related, are distinct).

PayPal gained notoriety for offering users $20 for signing up and an additional $20 for each referral, resulting in significant costs for the company through early VC subsidies. However, this substantial investment pales in comparison to the massive windfall of over $1 billion that Peter Thiel and Elon Musk received from eBay's acquisition.

The success of this strategy was not solely due to the $20 incentive, but rather because users had intrinsic motivations for bringing more users to the platform. It enhanced their experience by enabling them to send and receive money with more people, making the platform more valuable to them. Additionally, receiving an invitation from a trusted individual who wanted to send them money proved more persuasive than traditional advertising or cold emails. PayPal's simple yet effective referral strategy paved the way for exponential growth.

It is worth noting that Superchargers were not Musk's first encounter with network effects, as evidenced by PayPal, and they certainly won't be his last (RIP Twitter, welcome X?).

Facebook tellingly put now-billionaire Chamath Palihapitiya in charge of growth early on. He spearheaded initiatives like Facebook Connect that made it seamless to use your Facebook identity across third-party apps and sites. This increased lock-in by strengthening network bonds across the social graph, not to mention the simple utility for all parties—"Sign in with Facebook," one click where everybody wins. And with the interconnected profiles, the platform he helped build drove monetization through the Facebook ad network at scale. It wasn't just a good product, it made money. And created hundreds of billions in market cap.

But everybody starts at zero. As Andrew Chen described in his book *The Cold Start Problem*, overcoming early slow growth is imperative for startups—especially when they're trying to create a brand-new marketplace. Similar to Chamath, who was responsible for growth at Facebook, Chen was in charge of overseeing all aspects related to driver signup and the referral program at Uber. This led him to document the most challenging aspect of network effects—getting started. Here's the problem: how do you gain traction when starting from zero users or customers? VC firms are willing to absorb losses by subsidizing user acquisition and rapidly establishing critical network density because they understand the enterprise value of Metcalfe's and Reed's Laws.

But the startups they fund can't keep over-investing in user acquisition forever. Once the flywheel reaches a certain mass, network effects and word-of-mouth must generate outsized returns. Uber's node proximity and throughput, or liquidity (i.e., the ease of getting a ride when and where you need it), increased ride availability and reduced friction. Soon, network effects took over, creating an efficient and resilient market and competitive moat.

YouTube similarly jumpstarted scaling by building growth hooks into the product experience. Commenting, liking, and social kickbacks all nurtured network behavior. YouTube cemented itself as the hub for internet video by architecting social engagement and allowing creators access to their communities, creating a feedback loop to improve the products they shipped. Even though Netflix had a meteoric rise to the top of the streaming wars alongside YouTube, Netflix's walled garden approach eventually backfired. The darling of Silicon Valley—Netflix—is getting left behind.

While Netflix originally had high control over quality and was able to disrupt the traditional distribution of shows and movies through a better product, they were taught a painful lesson by YouTube and its parent, Google:

**Great product never beats great go-to-market. But great go-to-market never beats great network effects.**

The one with the network effects is seeing the payoff. Halfway through 2023, YouTube as a standalone product (not counting the rest of Alphabet's products or revenue) was growing revenue 62% faster than Netflix year over year, according to data from Variety.com and Macrotrends.net.

YouTube, as a platform and network, continues to grow its enterprise value without having to directly pay to acquire new users. YouTube has billions more users than Netflix (2.7B vs 238M at the time of writing), and now YouTube's revenue is forecasted to surpass Netflix's as well. With everyone entering the streaming wars, Netflix has little to differentiate itself from Disney, Hulu, Paramount, Max, Apple, and so on.

Being a "YouTuber" is a status symbol and a top career choice desired by Gen Z. Every creator is a node in YouTube's democratized content creation network where anyone can win, and everyone can win together. YouTube isn't just a product—it's an identity and a career. It's the most valuable content creator platform on the planet because of network effects.

Indeed, the "creator economy" is a household phrase. It's a dinner table conversation between kids and parents. That's the world we live in.

But at the same dinner table, would you ever hear a Gen Z kid talk about becoming a "Netflixer"? Nope. Not a single one. It seems that Netflix has forgotten about networks.

Across countless industries, eras, and examples, companies that recognize the exponential power of network effects win. They hardwire growth into their business model, strengthening network bonds, denser gravity, and widening throughput.

Remember, great product never beats great go-to-market. But great go-to-market never beats great network effects.

HipChat was a great product. Their competitor, Slack, was a slightly *different* product whose features weren't all that different from HipChat's when they first launched. But the real genius of Slack was in overlaying sales onto a product-led motion. Slack had a far superior GTM strategy and became a darling child of Silicon Valley with multiple ten figures of value. Rare air.

But, never, ever forget the network effects. HipChat met its demise at the hands of Slack's GTM. Slack dominated internal chat, until Slack met Teams. The story is so starkly clear as a visual you will never forget it:

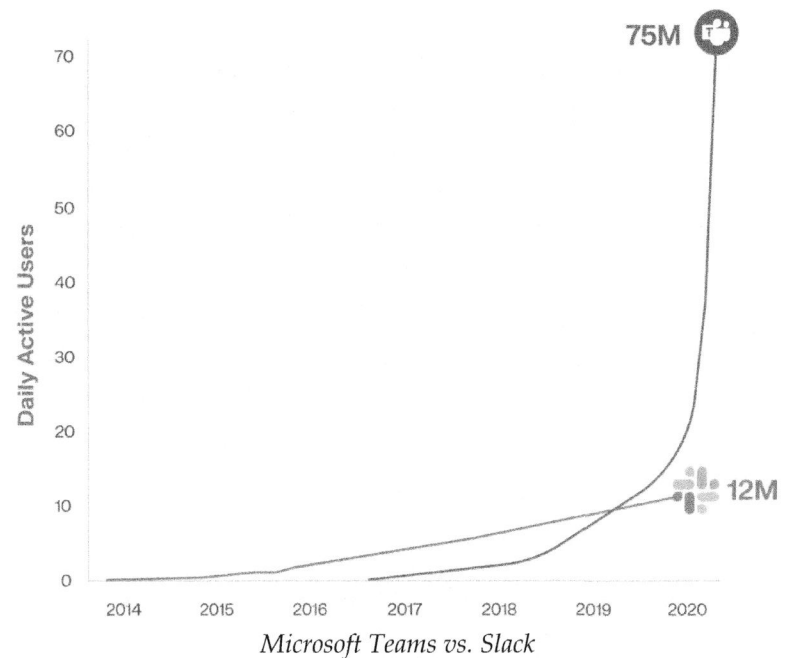

*Microsoft Teams vs. Slack*
**Source**: *Chartr.co, Company Announcements, VentureBeat, TechCrunch*

HipChat may have learned that great product never beats great GTM, but Microsoft taught everybody that great GTM never beats great network effects. The Microsoft ecosystem and nearbound mindset across every department absolutely dominated the productivity wars. As of 2022, according to BusinessofApps, Teams boasted 270M users compared to Slack's 18M. To win in the Nearbound Era, understanding and applying network effects is a necessity.

## Different Types of Network Effects

As previously mentioned, strategy is simply a choice. That's it. And not all choices are equal.

When it comes to laying the groundwork for nearbound it's important to understand the choices available to you in order to proactively recognize (and even create) network effects. And there's more than one type of network effect.

In fact, Currier's manual identifies 16 different types. We won't delve into all of his work here, but exploring some of them helps to set the stage for the strategic responsibilities that CEOs, founders, GTM executives, and partnership leaders have in this new era.

Some network effects are "direct," where value comes from other users, as we discussed with AT&T. Others are "indirect," attracting complementary providers. For instance, as more gamers purchased Xbox, more game developers joined the platform, creating a virtuous cycle that increased Xbox's value.

Two-sided marketplaces like Uber create unique network effects by coordinating distinct user groups. The diversity and nuance of modern network effects call for intentional orchestration.

Key modern network effects also include "social" effects, where users interact with other users, groups, and content, like on Facebook. And "data" effects, where collective information enhances solutions for all users, like YouTube's algorithms for consumers or LinkedIn for members.

Beyond direct and indirect effects, other fascinating types of network effects apply more than ever in the Nearbound Era.

### Language

Language has powerful network effects. Remember the example of "YouTuber" vs. "Netflixer"? Certain languages tend to dominate while others fade away. People in connected social, political, and economic networks converge around the same terms. English has become the global *lingua franca*, while regional languages have declined. The more speakers a language has, the more new speakers gravitate towards learning it.

## Bandwagon Effects

We also see bandwagon network effects that draw people in due to social pressure and fear of missing out. Slack leveraged this in the early days. Companies used it because employees already thought it was cool and they didn't want to miss out or be thought of as not with the times compared to competitors who used Slack.

## Ecosystem Effects

Notion demonstrates the utilization of ecosystem network effects. It created a marketplace for templates designed by its user community. Although Notion does not directly profit from template sales, the marketplace enhances the overall appeal of the platform. It attracts new users who discover Notion through viral TikTok videos that showcase templates while also providing existing users with added value and increasing customer retention.

Even teenagers can now monetize their creativity through Notion, showcasing the potential of architecting network effects that align incentives between businesses and their communities.

This self-reinforcing flywheel generates value for all parties involved in the network.

# Tear Down This Wall

In the Nearbound Era, network effects are everywhere—even as they remain understudied and are barely talked about in most MBA programs, much less company Zoom calls.

Their power stems not from scale but from intentional ecosystem design built into the company's GTM strategy from the outset. Scale is an output of network effects, not an input.

Merely having many users or partners does not guarantee compounding gains. This is the pitfall of siloing partnerships into a single department rather than baking it into your organization's DNA across every team.

Siloed partnership programs end up wasting precious time and resources on low-value one-off motions that never compound or generate flywheel effects. Why? Because these disjointed efforts aren't linked and leveraged within a diverse, self-perpetuating ecosystem and network.

As we explored with Tesla, network effects arise from cultivating **density, proximity, and throughput** as a hub within a broader ecosystem. Companies must architect *density* that creates gravity, pulling other entities into their orbit. Companies must build around where customers are, creating *proximity*. Companies must increase the *throughput* of the participants in the network, preserving trust to conserve time and money (the energy) of their system.

Effective ecosystems cannot be constructed through top-down decrees, slow death by outdated operating models, or a perfect org chart. They are intentionally orchestrated, but their effects emerge probabilistically when network incentives align between internal teams and external partnerships and relationships that surround the customer. Value accrues across varied, symbiotic relationships that reinforce one another.

That's why pioneering nearbound companies architect partnerships into the nervous system of the entire organization. They play long-term games focused on cultivating gravity through open ecosystems that attract partners into their flywheel.

Rather than optimize isolated metrics, they take a systems view. They recognize network incentives must be self-reinforcing: progress along one dimension enhances progress along others.

# The Nearbound Methodology: What You Need to Do Today

I'm going to sound like a broken record, but so be it: partnerships is not just a department, but an integrated strategy across every team.

The partnerships team should orchestrate connections for marketing, sales, customer success, product, and beyond. Rather than hoarding partner relationships, their responsibility is democratizing access company-wide. They tear down walls between teams both within the organization and outside of it, enabling the free flow of ideas and connections that were formerly segregated by the org chart.

As a leader, you need to *decide* to create watering holes where employees can congregate to exchange intelligence regardless of department.

Isaac Morehouse, my co-founder at nearbound.com, calls this the "Partner Pill." Once you take it, you can't stop seeing opportunities everywhere to tweak your strategy in line with the power of network effects built on trust.

I often refer to it as living in your zone of genius—when you work on something that has a positive impact on multiple other things. By doing one thing, you can impact five things, or fifty things, or five hundred.

There's a simple framework to help bring nearbound to every department, created with the help of Mark Kilens. Mark is the mastermind behind HubSpot's Inbound Academy, former VP of Community at Drift, CMO of Airmeet, and now Co-founder of Tack.

It's not complicated either. It's called ICE and it's pretty cool. (Get it? I couldn't help myself).

ICE stands for Identify, Collaborate, and Execute.

For every department, whether it's product, marketing, sales, success, or operations, incorporating nearbound motions requires the same three steps every time:

1. **Identify**: Determine who surrounds your buyer and who they trust. Identify potential partners that make sense to collaborate with. Establish connections with trusted partners to build a strong ecosystem of businesses working together. Use a Nearbound Revenue Platform (like Reveal!) to analyze overlaps with prospective partners and understand joint customer and prospect opportunities.
2. **Collaborate**: Align with partners on how you can provide mutual value to customers. Create joint marketing campaigns, co-branded content, and targeted events that generate mutual leads and drive pipeline. Utilize real-time insights from your Nearbound Revenue Platform to update target account lists based on partner overlap and customer statuses.
3. **Execute**: Take action to turn these relationships into results. Run specific plays to engage partners and their customers in the sales process. Leverage partner insights to gain valuable information, facilitate introductions, and influence customer decisions. Work with partners to ensure exceptional customer success and support, leading to high customer satisfaction, retention, and upsell opportunities. Utilize partner data to identify integration activation opportunities. Co-develop new products, services, or solutions with partners, utilizing shared expertise and resources to stay ahead of the competition and deliver value to customers.

Drilling down by department, the nearbound methodology enhances and expands the traditional responsibilities of each department as follows:

- **Marketing:** Partner marketing teams have typically focused narrowly on co-branded outlets. Nearbound aligns *all* demand-generation activities with ecosystem needs and realities. Content, events, and campaigns incorporate or highlight partners who add value for the audience.
- **Sales:** Alongside deal registration and lead passing, nearbound sales leverages trusted advisors to provide third-party validation

throughout the buying journey. Partners introduce new relationships, shape perceptions, and accelerate conversions.
- **Success:** Customer success has always depended on implementation partnerships to drive adoption. Nearbound strengthens these bonds by proactively re-engaging partners to maximize retention and expansion revenue.
- **Product:** Instead of viewing external technologies as threats, nearbound integrates them as value-adding complements through the platform. Cultivating stickiness through connections, not just features.

The remainder of this book will provide practical strategies, stories, and plays that can be executed *within each department*, as well as orchestrated across team borders. These strategies are designed to achieve quick wins and offset the diminishing returns of inbound and outbound approaches, all while playing the *infinite game*. These plays can help you reach your quarterly goals, satisfy your investors in the short term, and create a more stable business.

However, it's important to recognize that the true power of nearbound lies in the broader go-to-market decisions made by leaders. These decisions involve aligning your strategy with the market and positioning your company as a central node in a growing network, where the customer is constantly surrounded.

## A Final Note: Reaching Escape Velocity

Let me come back to Musk one more time. Just weeks after announcing Tesla's partnership with GM and Ford, he announced another pivotal partnership for SpaceX. Starlink is disrupting telecommunications at a mass scale with its partner, T-Mobile. If all goes according to plan, Starlink will soon be the most used internet connection on the planet.

Again, we see in this partnership strategic thinking. At PayPal, he partnered with eBay to power their payments. At Tesla, he partnered with Panasonic to build a better car battery. There's a clear pattern.

The moves we've discussed involve GM, Ford, Hilton, and T-Mobile, demonstrating a preference for massive partners and leveraging network effects in his biggest decisions. Like Warren Buffett, Musk is playing long-term games with long-term partners, focusing on a handful of big partnerships and decisions that will cement his impact on the industry. Isn't that the more exciting way to play?

Many people believe that Tesla's success is due to thousands of brilliant micro-level engineering insights and iterations. However, in reality, it is Musk's world-changing vision and go-to-market strategy that attract the talented individuals capable of making those innovations in the first place. His ecosystem approach provides the necessary resources, revenue, and network to continuously enhance the overall experience for the customers.

Whatever you think of him, Musk clearly understands the power of partnerships and ecosystems to unlock network effects.

So now we can see a slightly modified version of our adage: Great product never beats great go-to-market. But great go-to-market never beats *great partnerships that unlock* network effects.

This does not render product and engineering excellence irrelevant, just as embracing nearbound does not negate the importance of sales and marketing excellence. Outbound and inbound motions will still exist. However, focusing solely on them would be misguided when there are greater gains to be achieved in the nearbound realm.

Jill Rowley, one of the top salespeople and pioneers in the era of outbound and inbound automation, once told me:

> "I'm learning so much from partner professionals that I feel obligated to go back and re-educate the people I taught with the old GTM playbook. You still need lead nurturing, scoring, automation, and everything else. But I feel like I have to go back and say, 'That stuff was enough then, but now it's not enough. In this world, we need a lot more than that. We need to surround buyers with trust. We need nearbound."

Jill is one of the most influential B2B sellers of all time, largely credited with inventing "social selling." (We'll hear more from her later in this book.)

We stand at a pivotal juncture—between clinging to what worked previously and recognizing when to evolve. The nearbound frontier is closer than you imagined.

When you realize that buyers demand trust, that you need to partner with those surrounding them, and that creating a web of partners can unlock network effects, you are ready to enter the nearbound future.

Tear down the wall.

Break the silos of partnerships.

Let's go build the world where those who win, win together.

Time to get tactical.

# Part 2
## Nearbound Marketing

*"Marketers are increasingly focused on targeting the right accounts with the right message at the right time. Nearbound allows you to create a fuller picture of the influences that surround your buyer, and more effectively drive results by working with and through partners.*

*If you're trying to reach your market alone and only through direct means, you're going to run out of resources or get outcompeted by those who are tapping the power of their ecosystem."*

— Jessica Fewless

Director of Partnerships at Inverta, author of *Account-Based Marketing: How to Target and Engage the Companies That Will Grow Your Revenue*

## CHAPTER 3

# THE CURIOUS TASK OF MODERN MARKETING

The root of the word "marketing" is "market." But today, the practice of B2B marketing has strayed from its foundation—over-indexing on the "ing."

Without its roots, what is marketing?

Before we can answer that, we have to answer a more fundamental question: what is a market?

Encyclopedia Britannica describes it as follows:

> **Market**, a means by which the exchange of goods and services takes place as a result of buyers and sellers being in contact with one another, either directly or through mediating agents or institutions.

Markets, in the most literal sense, are places in which things are bought and sold. Yet, in the modern industrial system, a market transcends a physical space; it now encompasses the whole geographical area where sellers vie for customers. Alfred Marshall, known for his seminal work *Principles of Economics*, derived his definition of markets from French economist, A. Cournot:

"Economists understand by the term Market, not any particular marketplace in which things are bought and sold, but the whole of any region in which buyers and sellers are in such free intercourse with one another that the prices of the same goods tend to equality easily and quickly."

The interplay between economics and markets is so profound that Nobel laureate, Friedrich Hayek, even termed it the "market economy":

"[The] market economy [is] as an *information processing system* characterized by spontaneous order: the *emergence* of coherence through the independent actions of large numbers of individuals, each with limited and local knowledge, coordinated by prices that arise from decentralized processes of competition."

Hayek, one of my favorite economists, is known for his work on spontaneous order, monetary theory, and business cycles. But his deepest insight was a critique of those who attempted to interfere with natural emergent phenomena—what he called central planners. Their hubris rendered them victims of what Hayek termed "The Fatal Conceit."

The failures of totalitarian central planning are evident in the history of the 21st century, and Hayek provides piercing insight as to why those worldviews failed. The Fatal Conceit can be summed up in a Hayek quote I know by heart:

"The curious task of economics is to demonstrate to [all] how little they really know about what they imagine they can design."

This is crucial for understanding the difference between markets and marketing. Hayek's key tenet is that markets are emergent—not planned—and that they require actors to process information according to their own preferences and act accordingly. He contrasts the real dynamics of market actors and human action with the artificial mental models created by central planners. It's easy for ivory tower intellectuals to "math" the world they think they can create onto markets with policies, spreadsheets, and whitepapers. But these people don't make up markets. They don't drive economies. Actors **within** markets do.

Central planners might influence markets, but they do so through the opposite of consumer choice—they do it through laws or regulation. Something your marketing team likely doesn't have access to.

You've got to play the game fairly. This is a good thing. Not only does it force you to be sharper and more responsive to what creates value for customers, but winning through regulatory capture has unintended consequences that destroy value for all.

Bill Gurley, the notable founder of Benchmark, made this point clear in his *2,851 Miles* keynote at the 2023 All-In Summit when he said, "Regulation is the friend of the incumbent." He had the audience chanting because his examples hit home.

He showed that the goal of the *Telecommunications Act of 1996* was "to promote competition […] and encourage the rapid development of new telecommunications technologies."

But five years down the line, the exact opposite happened. In 1996, the top four telecom providers held 48% market share. Five years later, after successful lobbying efforts, the same four providers held 85% market share.

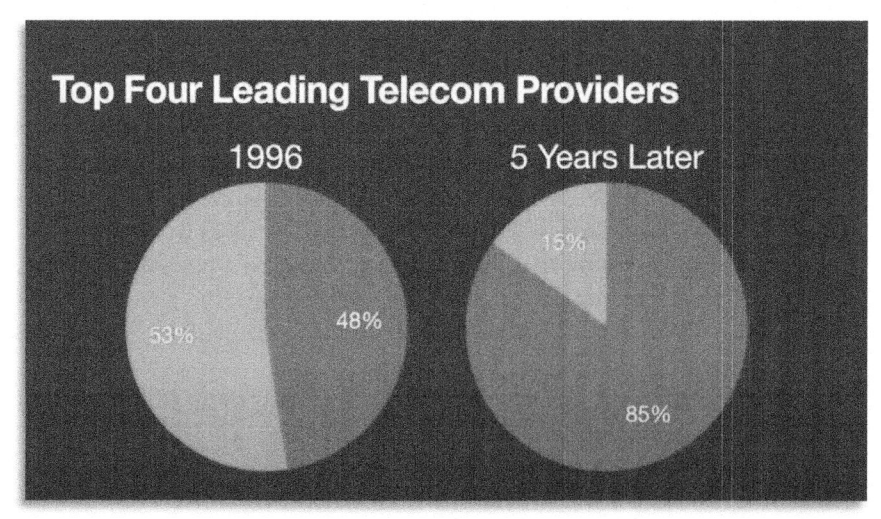

*Source: Bill Gurley presentation 2,851 Miles*

15% of all VC dollars used to go into telecom equipment innovation, but within 10 years, it dropped to less than 1%. It is so low now that it's no longer tracked:

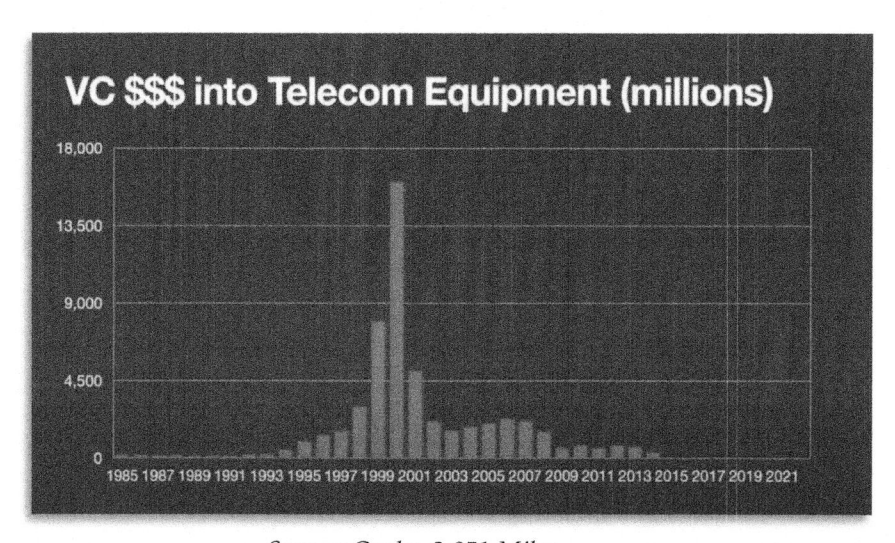

*Source: Gurley 2,851 Miles*

## THE CURIOUS TASK OF MODERN MARKETING

On both stated objectives, the bill that passed and the plans that were enacted from it did the exact opposite of their stated goals. The "curious task" indeed.

So, why open up the chapter on nearbound marketing with this point? Because the same phenomenon is happening in B2B. The B2B marketing plans being put to the market aren't having their desired effect.

Does your marketing strategy revolve around the idea of "imagining the world you think you can design"? Do you solely focus on measuring what happened and taking credit when the numbers align, but shift blame elsewhere when they don't? Does your model assume a predetermined vision or customer journey that you believe you can impose on the world? Unless you have the luxury of being able to lobby and create laws for your market based on your operating model and marketing metrics, it might be wise to reconsider your approach.

That's the curious task of marketing in the Nearbound Era: to demonstrate to the model makers, the funnel obsessives, the central planners, and ivory tower intellectuals just how little they know about what they imagine they can design. Don't fall into their trap.

I'm not here to tell you to discard everything about marketing operating models, data, funnels, or P&Ls. But I do want to remind you of a truth few like to acknowledge: your business exists in a market economy where you are not the central planner. Your marketing plan is not absolute. You are a participant in the market. Your market-*ing* is not your model. Your market-*ing* is the sum of all information being processed by the market. Whether through sign-ups, conversations, rumors, referrals, or signed contracts, your marketing is inherently larger than individual activities, campaigns, or funnel calculations.

The act of marketing is based on imperfect information. People act in ways you could never plan or imagine. Even the best available data, though valuable, can never provide the full picture. As Alfred Korzybski eloquently put it, "The map is not the territory."

Your map is not the territory. Your model is not the market.

What, then, is the territory?

Human action.

It's about what is happening to and by the humans who could, would, or did buy your product. It's about observing their complete and comprehensive picture over time, not just the small sliver that you can measure about yourself in relation to them.

Hayek's Nobel Prize-winning first principles can't teach you how to do modern marketing. But they can teach you something far more important: what *not* to do. They can teach you to participate—to step down from the ivory tower and observe what is happening on the streets.

They can teach you to recognize when your own actions as a consumer do not align with your assumptions as a marketer. And, of course, they can teach you to see the world through the eyes of your current and potential customers.

At the root of marketing is the study of human action in your market. Ludwig von Mises, a fellow Austrian economist, and author of the magnum opus *Human Action*, referred to this study as "praxeology."

My Co-founder, Isaac Morehouse, and I have been students of human action and how it works in markets for over 15 years. It's how we met each other. In fact, Isaac's first startup was called Praxis (you can guess where he got the name). These first principles run deep in us—we're geeks for them.

When you view the world from the perspective of human behavior, you spend less time thinking about what you imagine you can design and work on what is actually happening *in* the market with the market participants. It's humbling, but also exciting. The world is full of wonder and we're always trying to keep up. Because, at the end of the day, the market always wins.

The curious task of modern marketing is not about throwing away everything you think you know. It's about becoming obsessed with your customers and their desired experiences. Who they are, who they trust, where they hang out, what they do, and why. What's changing, and what's staying the same?

It's not enough to target or attract the customers you want. Nearbound marketing is about surrounding them where they are and alongside those they trust.

It's time to put the *market* back in marketing.

## CHAPTER 4

# THE NEW CMO

Allison Munro is the Chief Market & Ecosystem Officer at Vena Solutions. Notice her title. She's not just a CMO as you may know it; she's the Chief "Market" Officer. And the ecosystem extension is intentional, too, but we'll get to that. On a typical day, Allison receives 25-50 prospecting emails and 10+ cold LinkedIn messages, just like every other executive.

What does she do with these? She ignores them. Like most executives, she doesn't really have a choice.

"I probably have 75+ unread messages in my inbox every day, and I do not answer my phone if I see a number that I do not know," she told me back in November of 2022.

I can relate. I recently counted a record 45 cold calls to my personal cell phone... before noon. With a majority of companies using disruptive market-*ing* tactics instead of *living in market*, the "Silence Unknown Callers" feature has become indispensable.

And if it's happening to me, *it's happening to your buyers.*

I invited Allison onto my podcast to talk about what it means to be an ecosystem-oriented Chief Market Officer. Her own plight on the receiving end of these tactics illustrates the untenable position that CMOs now face.

"Buyers have become almost unreachable," she said.

Allison continued that we can't look at how we respond to the tactics we're targeted with, only to go replicate them because an activity model said so. The map we're trying to design doesn't match the territory. Our marketing doesn't match the human behavior of the market.

It's no surprise, then, that CMOs are under immense pressure. Their average tenure is the shortest of any executive role, just 18 months in the position. And it's not just human action that's causing the shift— macroeconomic realities are setting in, too.

In the wake of the 2023 recession, marketing budgets were cut when CEOs and boards realized that Customer Acquisition Cost (CAC) was only increasing with more spend. Chris Walker, the gadfly of attribution and father of "dark social," broke it down like this: he analyzed the 2022 advertising benchmark study by metadata.io across $42MM in advertising spend and 236,000 leads converted. His takeaways are hard to accept, just like the hard boardroom conversations happening right now.

Chris found that 90% of all advertising dollars were spent on lead generation campaigns. "Download" was the most popular call-to-action (CTA), indicating that gated PDFs were still the number one offer. The average cost to get someone to read a PDF through advertising on Facebook or LinkedIn? $126 for a download. And based on the exact same data set, he estimated the win rate to be 0.3% from that cohort of leads. This means that sales needs 333 "leads" to win ONE deal. But even if you accept the average cost per lead as reasonable, that map isn't the territory. The full picture is worse.

Chris continued:

> "[T]he average cost per "lead" was $172 across all lead gen campaigns. [Given the] low win rate of these leads, we estimate advertising CAC to be **$57,000** to win one deal. This is just the advertising cost and doesn't include sales headcount, SDRs, marketing headcount, or other marketing programs such as events. It's safe to say this performance is totally unacceptable."

$57,000. And CAC payback is getting worse, too. Chris broke down the study further to conclude:

"When you include all the other expenditures, you could reasonably estimate the total CAC payback on these programs is more than 48 months (meaning it takes 4 years just to pay back the cost of acquiring the customer, not adjusted for gross margin). $38MM in total advertising spend on lead gen campaigns resulting in $22MM in closed won revenue."

Paid spend for lead generation has hit an inflection point. Even if you are a top performer, the aggregate is moving in the wrong direction.

When it comes to organic search, it's not any easier. Google dominates the first page of every relevant keyword and even provides in-line generative AI answers from Bard. This is helpful for users, but it presents a challenge for publishers and content creators who rely on SEO, especially compared to social media. In 2021, renowned SEO entrepreneur, Rand Fishkin, conducted a study revealing that 65% of all Google searches end without a click, up from 50% in 2019. With the introduction of Google Bard results displayed in-line, it's anyone's guess where the percentage of searches that end in clicks will end up.

While the data on this isn't quite in, I can say it has changed the way I search since I started using Chrome as my default browser. Before GPT 4 Pro, my default Chrome tabs (stored as pinned tabs for quick access) included Gmail, Calendar, Drive, and various other pinned sites based on my primary focus at the time, such as Clari, Salesforce, HubSpot, PandaDoc, or Drift. However, Gmail was always my first tab (accessible via tab 1 or cmd+1). Somehow, GPT has replaced it. I'm not even sure when or how, but it has become my go-to.

Regarding mobile, the "dock" on my iPhone has remained unchanged since my first one: Phone, iMessage, Email, Safari. Interestingly, and I don't remember doing it, Safari has been replaced by OpenAI's ChatGPT native app. I still use Safari on mobile, of course, but it is no longer my default.

Sure, that's just me. But it's instructive. Very few things in tech last, but my pattern—using the same productivity apps in the same order—lasted over a decade. When something that has been standing for so long changes it's worth thinking about. How we act governs what the data about our behavior is supposed to capture. But the data doesn't govern how we act. Accordingly, investing in organic content reliant on SEO is no longer the growth lever it once was. Behavior is changing. I don't search, I ask. I don't click, I ask again. And I'll never revert back to the baseline of old search. It doesn't seem like the rest of the market will either.

In B2B, there are fewer places to get in front of buyers without paying a toll, and that toll is going up all the time. Budgets are down. Paid is becoming prohibitively expensive. Organic is becoming increasingly less effective. CMOs and marketers, I feel you. The B2B playbook we grew up with in the Outbound and Inbound Eras aren't mapping to the territory.

## Marketing in the Who Economy

Let's return to the shift in buying behavior we described in the introduction—the transition from the How Economy to the Who Economy.

In the How Economy, companies competed to get information in front of the right people at the right time.

In the Who Economy, companies battle for influence around their customers. But where does influence come from? It's certainly not from viral, flash-in-the-pan posts or swanky celebrity sponsorships.

**True influence comes from trust, and trust comes from those who help.**

We don't have the room or resources to waste on salesy pitches and interruptions. We only have room for proof, and, as the data shows, the best proof comes from those we already have a relationship with.

Buyers are hungry for people who've already walked the path to success. They are seeking out people who have been where they want to go or who have helped them before. We need our own people's proof, not just your words.

This is what nearbound leverages; it's about connecting **the right people to people** and should be integrated into every strategy and department in your organization. No place is more critical or powerful than the marketing department.

As a marketer, when was the last time you Googled how to solve a marketing automation problem? I bet you don't ask Google *how* to do something as much as you used to. Instead, I bet you ask questions like "Who can I ask that has already done this successfully?" or "Who is like me that's done this before?"

Even review sites don't factor into purchasing decisions the way they used to. I've been on some public rants in the past couple of years about what I call "4.7-star syndrome." Every review we seem to look at has 4.7 stars! The magic number! 4.9 and it must be fake, 4.4 and it must be trash. So magically, 4.7 is the number we see everywhere. But when everyone is rated 4.7 stars and everyone has badges, accolades, or reviews, do buyers care?

Much to my surprise, one of my rants on LinkedIn about the "4.7-star syndrome" drew the attention of TrustRadius CEO, Vinay Bhagat. When I saw him join the conversation, I was shocked to hear him say that he agreed! How could even the CEO of one of the most trusted review sites agree with my hot take on the "4.7-star syndrome"?

Turns out, he didn't just agree with the 4.7-star syndrome. He agreed on the rise of the Who Economy. He kindly offered a 1-1 conversation with me, where I learned about a recent study his team published on a survey of 2,000 B2B buyers. That call was a pivotal moment for me. I knew in my heart that we weren't using review sites like we used to, but his survey results were so eye-opening that even I was shocked. I booked him immediately for episode 123 of the Nearbound Podcast because this story had to be told.

Here's just a snapshot of what he shared from the survey:

According to buyers, the most important factor of a review site is "Reviewers relatable to me." In fact, the factor of 'who' is exactly 230% more important than the overall score! Oh, and those badges and awards that are prominently displayed on your site, social media, and review pages? Well, they are precisely 2,300% less important than 'who.'

**Most Important Evalutation Factors on Review Sites for Buyers**

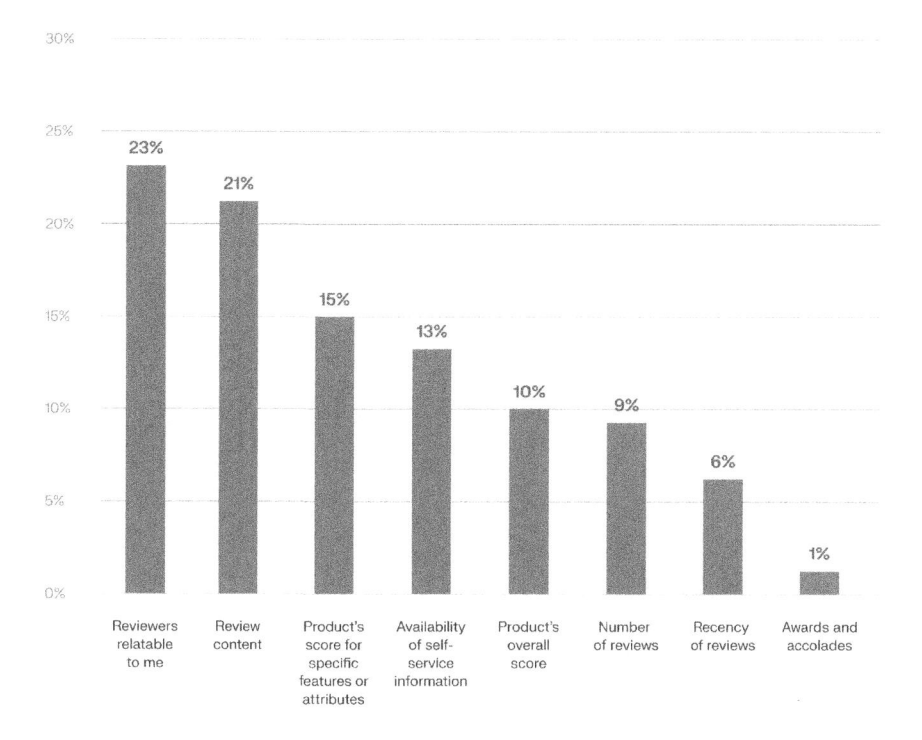

| Factor | Percentage |
|---|---|
| Reviewers relatable to me | 23% |
| Review content | 21% |
| Product's score for specific features or attributes | 15% |
| Availability of self-service information | 13% |
| Product's overall score | 10% |
| Number of reviews | 9% |
| Recency of reviews | 6% |
| Awards and accolades | 1% |

*Source: TrustRadius 2023 Buying Disconnect Study. Sample size: 2,000*

As both buyers and professionals, we no longer seek aggregate information online; we seek direct advice from trusted relationships and proven experts whom we can reference relevant to our specific situation. Vinay and his team at TrustRadius are honest in surfacing the facts given the hyper-relevancy of their data set to their market, despite the counterintuitive position it could place their product in. Our buying journeys are shaped by the people we know and admire, people like us but in a future state. People to whom we can see ourselves being in a future state and to whom we most relate. Our searches lead us to the advice and input of real, flesh-and-blood friends, individuals, fellow community members, influencers, and people like us—not faceless websites. Buyer preferences changed in the Who Economy—but if you used a review site, you already knew that too. You want "who" not "how."

Today's CMOs must shift their focus from solely determining "how" to reach the market, to identifying "who" can help them reach their desired goals, just like their potential customers do. This question sets the stage for the nearbound approach of marketing *with* instead of marketing *to*.

## Marketing *With*: The Soul of Nearbound

The nearbound marketing playbook is still being written, and it's a refreshing mix of different and familiar. The fundamentals of marketing that have been forgotten in the rush of the digitization and automation eras are making a major comeback.

While outbound *targets* and inbound *attracts*, nearbound *surrounds* and *connects* through trusted relationships. Developing any content, campaign, or event that does not involve people buyers already trust is playing on hard mode.

Nearbound marketing means marketing *with* people who already have relationships and operate in the same spaces as your target audience. Instead of asking, "How can I sell my product?", nearbound asks, "Where are my buyers, and whom do they trust?"

The answer to this will dictate how you organize internally, as well.

I will keep repeating it: trust comes from helping people reach their promised land. And those best suited to help are the ones who have been there. I cannot overstate the profundity of the paradox this creates for your marketing team:

> If trust comes from helping people reach their promised land and that's best done by people who have already been there, how can we expect people to trust us when we haven't?

To earn trust, we must help people achieve their goals. When making purchases today, we seek guidance from those who have already achieved the goals we are striving for.

Again, let's say your company's buyers are Chief Information Officers. *How many people on your marketing team have ever been a CIO?*

Marketers alone cannot help a CIO become a better CIO because they've never been one, much less one who has solved the challenges faced by their target CIOs. The partners and communities where they live can provide such help. Market with those people.

The heart and soul of nearbound marketing is paved on the path to your buyers' promised land. If you've never walked your buyers' path, you better partner with those who have.

## What's Old is New Again: How to Win Customers and Influence People

The goal of nearbound marketing is building trust, not merely maximizing reach. It focuses on becoming part of the conversation by highlighting partners, advocates, and creators. Proximity and influence are built through serving others versus promoting yourself.

Every industry, subculture, and field of inquiry has its influencers. These individuals are kings in the Who Economy. But it's not just the MrBeasts of the world, with multi-million-dollar YouTube empires, who influence the buyer's journey. It's anyone your buyer trusts—whether that's advisors, advocates, customers, or partners.

As I've already emphasized, the idea of leveraging relationships and influencers is not new—it's a return to what worked before the digital era. In the past, business relationships were cultivated on golf courses and over martini lunches, and through massive billboard campaigns of the Brand Era. But today, we look beyond celebrity endorsements to seek out expertise from people who have been to our promised land and can guide us to where we aim to go.

B2B is no exception. Influencers, evangelists, and brand ambassadors are prevalent, even in the outbound industry. Take Ryan Reisert, for example. He co-authored the bestselling book *Outbound Sales, No Fluff*, and served as the Founder & CEO of Phone Ready Leads before its acquisition. With his extensive experience in cold calling, outbound sales, and data, Ryan became a Brand Ambassador for Cognism, a sales intelligence company valued at $436 million in 2023. What made Ryan an effective brand ambassador was not his employee status, but his relevance. Having made countless cold calls himself, people trusted his voice. Salespeople rely on individuals like Ryan who have firsthand experience and knowledge, rather than anonymous reviewers or actors pretending to be experts. It's ironic that even in the outbound industry, cold callers and data companies leverage nearbound marketing to influence buyers.

Some teams attempt a surface-level version of this by paying for brand exposure through creators or communities. They call it a partnership, but often it is just paying for their logo to be put on something. Nearbound marketing requires actually participating in markets authentically, not just marketing to them transactionally.

Rather than one-off sponsorships, the ideal nearbound marketing relationships evolve into a valuable two-way flow of knowledge, traffic, and people. A distinction between nearbound marketing and brand marketing is the flow of knowledge. Your partners should not merely be distribution channels, but collaborators in creating and serving your collective audience with useful information. A simple example of this could be quoting a partner in an area of their expertise, such as in an article or guide, getting their input along the way, versus creating it and passing it over to be distributed to their audience.

The "watering holes" concept provides a mental model for understanding this distinction. A watering hole is a place where your audience already gathers, such as forums, events, podcasts, and social media clusters. You can interview thought leaders at industry watering holes or co-host events with partners who share your values. The goal is to become part of your audience's conversations without interrupting them—done right, you're participating *with* them, not marketing *to* them.

Before crafting marketing content or campaigns, always consider: where do my buyers go and who do they already trust? The focus should be on surrounding your audience with proximity, not promoting your product out of context.

## When the Going Gets Tough

When the pandemic hit just months after Allison became CMO at Vena, she didn't wait around to see how her field would adapt. She started to take risks—rethinking her role in the context of partnership ecosystems. At the time, there was no playbook for nearbound, or even the language to talk about it.

As of March 2020, Vena had been planning a huge 7,000-person in-person event which was effectively canceled by the lockdowns. Many would have used the circumstances of COVID-19 as an excuse to tamp down expectations from leadership. Allison took it as a calling to take her curiosity about ecosystems into the realm of courageous action. Rather than canceling the event, they pivoted to a virtual format—a first for Vena. They focused on immersing themselves in the market and creating conversations with trusted voices. The event ended up spawning an entirely new Learning Academy. Soon after, they launched a forum and became one of the go-to watering holes for Excel nerds.

"Everyone was focusing on maybe pulling back and pausing," Munro told me. "We were like, 'No, we're going all in on our community.'"

Three years later, Allison is now Chief *Ecosystems* Officer at Vena. She has begun to author the marketing playbook of the Nearbound Era while her peers sweat at the prospect of where they will ply their outmoded trade come 2025.

Today, it's riskier to ignore the changes in the market than to continue with the old demand generation tactics. My dad was fond of telling my siblings and me, "When the going gets tough, the tough get going." It seems cliché, but you have to do something different in this market.

Tell your story with the people who your customers already trust.

## CHAPTER 5

# SURROUND SOUND MARKETING IN 5 PHASES

Let's review the core principles of nearbound marketing:

- Recognizing markets as emergent processes, which exist prior to our market-*ing* activities.
- Participating in ecosystems and building loyalty through relationships first.
- Surrounding your audience with influence.
- Marketing *with* the relevant influencers rather than marketing *to* your customers.

We will do well to keep these principles top of mind as we shift from concepts to tactics—from theory to practice.

By participating in markets first, many of the necessary tactics will become clear organically. But when you've never attempted to live in market before, it can feel risky. When you're accustomed to marketing *to* prospective customers, marketing *with* partners can take you out of your comfort zone.

There are two ways to run nearbound marketing at a tactical level:

1. **Underlay:** Change your GTM to be nearbound from the ground up
2. **Overlay:** Layer nearbound onto your existing activities

## SURROUND SOUND MARKETING IN 5 PHASES

The first is a native-to-nearbound approach that requires a more fundamental shift. This approach does not regard your current headcount, campaigns, plans, or activities as sacred. You may need to change the rhythm of how you run your business. It's probably best suited to companies without a mature marketing team and processes.

But there's also a simple overlay framework you can use to bring nearbound plays into your existing activities right now, with no major changes to the way you run your business.

This chapter will provide an in-depth roadmap to the overlay model, while the next chapter will provide a framework for the most tactical takeaways to get you started.

To make nearbound marketing more approachable, my partner Isaac Morehouse and Logan Lyles, host of the *Nearbound Marketing* podcast, created a useful 5-phase system:

1. Defining Your ICP (Ideal Customer Profile)
2. Establishing a Strategic Narrative
3. Assembling a Nearbound Marketing Team
4. Activating Your Evangelists
5. Iterating and Scaling

While the first two phases cover best practices that will be familiar to veteran marketing professionals, steps three through five take you into the future of nearbound marketing—getting tactical about activating influencers and evangelists surrounding your buyer.

They've had hundreds of conversations with B2B marketing leaders on nearbound and have been running these plays as much as anyone. Their framework aims to help you de-risk the process by providing adaptable, actionable steps.

Done well, this approach creates a reliable growth engine powered by networks of trust and influence—not a faucet-style funnel to be turned on or off.

This system is based on their years of collective marketing, partnerships, and sales experience, and more importantly, the experience and expertise of others they've spoken with. It isn't Ivory Tower academics or business schools teaching you about marketing. Instead, it focuses on what they have observed to be effective and the commonalities that lead to success.

Let's dive in.

# Phase 1: Defining Your ICP—Niche Down to Create Resonance

The first phase of nearbound marketing involves narrowing your Ideal Customer Profile (ICP) as much as possible.

Most companies start too broad. They say, "Our customers are manufacturers in North America with 100 to 1,000 employees."

But your ICP should niche down further than demographics. Your ICP needs to answer not only what accounts, but also what *partners* and *vendors* you trust. The 'who' that surrounds the ICP.

Start by analyzing your current top accounts and partners—those with the highest adoption, usage, lifetime value (LTV), or longest retention—to uncover patterns. What technographic commonalities emerge? In other words, examine which tools and software are most used in the tech stacks of your top accounts. This technographic data in particular is crucial and highlights the other technology companies you can market with to reach your buyers where they are.

You should also identify "lighthouse" clients that perfectly represent your ICP. These are the cream of the crop—the people who buy the quickest, stay the longest, and become the biggest advocates. Build marketing specifically for these niche personas and buyers. The narrower your niche, the better your marketing will be.

For example, in his role as Evangelism & Content Marketing at Teamwork.com, Logan observed that their target audience was not simply CEOs in general, but specifically CEOs at a particular stage in their career who approach operations in a specific manner. These psychographic attributes are what make them a good fit, and they hold more significance than geography in the post-pandemic world, where remote work is breaking down the remaining barriers to globalization.

Next, let actual sales conversations with customers and prospects shape your marketing messaging rather than vice versa.

As marketers, we love forming a radical point of view, creating frameworks and language, designing campaigns, and creating content. We come up with the messaging and give it to the sales team. But what if we started in reverse—working with partners or talking to your (prospective) customers and letting the conversations dictate the marketing message? Real people tend to have more specific needs than the faceless ICP figures we conjure up.

These questions can be as simple as:

- What's your biggest win to date?

- What is your biggest challenge/pain point?
- What are your goals for the next quarter? The next year?
- What's the biggest blocker for reaching those goals?
- Who in the industry do you look to for advice, or as an example of success?
- Who is helping you execute your vision that's not on your team? What service providers, communities, or tech do you turn to in order to make calls you need to make?
- What do you read or listen to every day/week?

To do nearbound marketing right, you need to be able to answer quickly and clearly not just, "Who is my ideal customer," but also, "Who does my ideal customer trust?"

## Phase 2: Establishing a Strategic Narrative—Make Yourself Easy to Market With

Phase 2 involves developing a strategic narrative—an overarching brand story and positioning related to your customer's point of view.

The "strategic narrative" concept was popularized by Andy Raskin, the go-to guru for Silicon Valley leadership teams who are trying to reframe company strategy as a company story.

Raskin has laid out five steps to developing a strategic narrative:

1. Name a big, relevant change in the world
2. Show that there will be winners and losers
3. Tease the promised land
4. Introduce features as "Magic Gifts" for overcoming obstacles to the promised land
5. Offer evidence that you can make the story come true

In marketing, it's easy to focus solely on what our company or product is. But it's important to remember that it's not just about the features and benefits; it's about the outcomes. What does it look like when you achieve success? Your company or product is not the hero of the story but rather an enabler that helps your prospects get to where they want to be.

Rather than deciding on a top-down overarching story right away, start by uncovering your authentic customer point of view through public testing. Again, let real discussions with partners and evangelists inform your narrative and shape your messaging. Put out iterations of your ideas and use comments as feedback loops. "Building in public" is just another way of saying "living in the market," or as Isaac likes to say, "learning out loud."

People want to learn from and trust those who have already achieved success in the area they are trying to break into or are currently struggling with. That's why it's important to connect with individuals who have been through or are seeing the same journey to serve as a relatable example for your audience. Your marketing should incorporate the real people you've helped in your narrative—and the people who surround them—from people who have used your product and advised their customers to solve their problems.

Pete Caputa, the agency program creator at HubSpot and CEO at Databox I referred to earlier, provides an excellent example of someone who learned from partners before shaping strategic messaging.

As discussed in Chapter 2, Pete pioneered an innovative agency partner program during his early days at HubSpot. Having previously run his own agency, he understood the challenges that small and medium agencies faced first-hand.

Rather than pushing HubSpot's product—a CMS platform—Caputa focused on enabling agencies to build better businesses. He helped agencies specialize around particular client niches to drive more predictable revenue streams. This involved leveraging HubSpot's primary capabilities to continually create new content that clients would pay for on a recurring basis. By prioritizing *partner* needs, Caputa cultivated genuine relationships that drove rapid growth. HubSpot's agency business grew from $0 to $100 million under Caputa's leadership.

This initial success was powered by Caputa's partner-centric mindset coupled with a compelling narrative shaped directly from insights into partners' worlds. Before detailing HubSpot's solutions, Caputa took the time to understand agencies' goals and roadblocks. This empathy allowed HubSpot to position itself as an ally rather than just another software vendor.

Like Caputa, you need to understand the entire ecosystem surrounding your potential buyers. Before crafting your narrative, picture your buyer surrounded by orbiting planets, each with its own proximity and gravitational pull around them. These orbiting planets represent all the nodes that influence them. Mapping this out can help you identify who all those nodes are, including partners, customers, and others.

The proximity and gravitational pull will differ based on factors like authority, trust, business impact, and frequency of communication. Mapping out these planetary bodies illuminates exactly who you need to learn from and serve. Again, this doesn't have to be rocket science. *Talk* to your top (and future) customers and ask them who they turn to.

While end customers should remain the priority, the second focus must be on those orbiting partners. By enabling partners rather than simply promoting to them, you empower an extension of yourself. When they succeed, you succeed. Equip partners to better serve customers, and gravitational pull brings all three bodies into tighter, faster-spinning orbits around one other.

Marketers are used to prioritizing customers first and their own product second. The customer is first, that much is correct. But after customers, it's those they trust—your partners—followed by your story and, finally, your product.

Rather than viewing partners as just another distribution channel, recognize them as the center of gravity. Enable them to better understand and serve *their* customers, and their orbit pulls *your* prospects into alignment.

At Databox, Caputa continues applying his signature partner-first approach to growth. Databox's Benchmark Groups enable partners to instantly benchmark their clients' performance against competitor companies in their niche.

Rather than claiming broad expertise across industries, Databox arms partners with data to quantify their specialty. It's brilliant. Partners create targeted benchmark groups, comparing metrics from over 70 software tools used by similar businesses across innumerable segments of likeness.

This partner-first approach creates a positive feedback loop. More benchmark studies drive demand for integrating additional niche data sources. Those enhanced integrations then provide fuel for future benchmarking, partnerships, and co-marketing campaigns. As Caputa summarized, "Benchmark data is what turns a pro services firm that takes orders from clients—to one that gives the orders."

Databox has deliberately focused on network effects and tight ecosystem alignment from the start. Today, that strategy is compounding returns. Databox has cemented itself as one of HubSpot's most successful integration partners while also nurturing partnerships across the broader software landscape.

And Caputa is just getting started. With continual plans to work with more net new partners every month, the Databox flywheel continues to grow to surround new prospective customers with voices they trust. Helping agencies get to their promised land by equipping them to show *customers* how to get to theirs is the epitome of nearbound strategic narrative crafting.

# Phase 3: Assembling a Nearbound Marketing Team

While portions of the first two phases may be familiar to some marketers, they remind us of the key mindset shift: marketing *with* partners versus merely throwing marketing *at* them and expecting them to market *to* their customers.

In Phase 3, we build the core Marketing team needed to activate evangelists and surround buyers with trusted voices. Rather than just hiring top marketing talent at a premium, the nearbound approach leverages four unique personas:

1. Journalists
2. Content creators
3. Partners
4. Customers

They don't need to be directly on your payroll either. Instead, you can set up revenue share agreements or other win-win arrangements to expand your reach without increasing your number of employees.

Let's break down the four key roles in a nearbound marketing team, and the core jobs to be done by each.

## Journalists

**Job to be done:** Story *finding*

First, bring in journalists who excel at uncovering stories—discerning signal through the noise—and spotting trends from the market without bias. Their skills in investigatory interviewing and story-finding from the mundane are invaluable. Journalists help your team approach the market without preconceptions, gathering insights that may contradict your own views or pre-existing story. Having a journalist on your team prevents your messaging from becoming too insular. A good journalist knows what it means to live in market, and they can help you identify customer watering holes if you're having trouble.

The good news is that the journalism industry has been disrupted, and many talented journalists are underpaid in their current positions. Logan, for example, was a journalist before pivoting into sales, before pivoting again into marketing. He notes that marketing people talk a lot about storytelling but much less about story *finding*. This is an essential skill to have on the marketing team of the future.

You don't need to position yourself or your company as the expert if you can find the experts already trusted by your buyers and pull stories out of them.

## Creators

**Job to be done:** Story *spreading*

For the next persona, you want to partner with authentic content creators who already produce material your target buyers love. As we've discussed, buyers identify most with creators who have been in their shoes and can relate to their challenges—those who have been to their promised land. Look especially for creators who speak about their personal experiences. Their relatable stories and advice will attract and retain buyers better than generic product marketing.

You can leverage creators both internally and externally. For example, enable team members with creator potential to build their personal brands. Or, collaborate on content with industry influencers who attract your ideal customers. But you must make it easy for people to market with you. That may involve learning to write drafts for people in their own voice that are so good they can share them with little to no editing. Creators and influencers often have more willingness than bandwidth to co-create with you. The better you can capture their voice and get them workable concepts, language, and copy, the better.

As an aside, this is something that's hard for AI to replicate or disrupt. As more companies seek to scale content with AI, the genuinely human stuff stands out even more. That being said, some content creators have started using AI + the human as a workflow for these kinds of tasks. You can feed ChatGPT samples of a person's writing style you are trying to imitate along with the bullet points of the content you want to put in their words to help replicate this at scale.

## Partners

**Job to be done:** Story *connecting*

From service partners to technology partners to referral partners, they all have relationships with audiences you want to reach. More importantly, they have audiences that you can help them teach. Instead of directly promoting your product, help them craft stories about their customers' journey to success, portraying them as heroes.

The best marketing teams and programs are those where you "make your partners famous," as Caputa puts it. You are the set designer, makeup artist, and producer all in one. Make the content so good that it can't help but gather a crowd and attract more partners to the show.

Make partners proud to share your content because it makes them look good.

**Customers**

**Job to be done:** Story *validating*

Finally, your team should engage with customers who have achieved success using your product. These customers add a layer of credibility when sharing your brand story. Their living endorsements serve as valuable social proof, which goes beyond static testimonials or case studies.

Here's the reality: if the only time your customers are promoting your brand is in your case studies, then you're approaching marketing the wrong way. Instead, position your marketing efforts where your customers are, not just where you want them to be. If they are actively discussing topics related to your brand on social media, then engage with them on social media. Attend events that your customers frequent. Be present in the same market as your customers. Engage with them in communities, through owned media, podcasts, studies, and more. Wherever your customers reside, make sure you are there too.

Your customers aren't just chunks of revenue to retain; they are partners. They live in the market, and a good nearbound marketer makes it easy for them to talk about you with their peers.

***

Sometimes the lines blur between these personas. You might find content creators who are former buyers of your product, or who have solved the same problem, or those who were customers whom you could help become content creators, or partners who are customers and content creators. These roles are not necessarily embodied by specific individuals but are rather personas.

By combining the approaches, your marketing team can more readily activate partners and other evangelists surrounding your buyer. The result is an orchestrated surround sound marketing strategy, amplifying voices of trust to your audience.

## Phase 4: Activate Your Evangelists

Activating your network of evangelists is the crucial step that brings the inbound marketing methodology to life. An evangelist is not a title but rather any sort of influencer to a potential buyer who shares your vision of the promised land—it includes the personas mentioned above but extends even further.

This phase focuses on identifying and collaborating with the nodes of trust already orbiting your ideal customer. The goal is earning attention and, ultimately, loyalty through relevance and relationships.

If you nail Phase 4, you ignite a self-reinforcing virtuous cycle. You've heard of flywheels versus funnels—this is where the perpetual motion begins. Your evangelists gain prominence, which expands their reach and influence. This compounds your collective authority in the market as you converge into a movement with momentum.

Chances are you already have an army of potential evangelists around you, even if you don't know it yet.

To make the rubber meet the road, Isaac and Logan break this down into five smaller steps.

## Step 1: Identify Potential Evangelists

The first step in activating your evangelists is to examine the broader market and ecosystem surrounding your ideal customer. The goal is to identify individuals and organizations that already have influence and are trusted by your audience.

These are your potential evangelists—the key voices you'll ultimately want to draw from and activate to amplify your messaging and strategic narrative. Evangelists come in two forms: internal and external.

Internally, think about subject matter experts across departments like customer success, engineering, and product development. These folks have incredible insight into your customers' pain points and desires from their day-to-day interactions. Your executives can also lend gravitas and leadership credibility as internal evangelists.

Externally, explore partnerships with industry advisors, content creators, agencies, investors, and existing happy customers.

Create a list of your internal and external evangelists—anyone who surrounds your buyer and whom they trust. These individuals don't necessarily have to be partners, although partners are a great starting point due to the already-established formal relationships. Moreover, partner managers are often ready and waiting for marketers to connect with them and begin collaborating.

Ask your partner managers, "Who are some of our top partners? With whom should we organize an event this quarter, or collaborate on advertisements, content, etc.?"

The goal of nearbound marketing is to weave together best practices from partner marketing, influencer engagement, and customer advocacy—familiar concepts in the modern marketing handbook—into an integrated strategy.

## Types of potential evangelists:

| INTERNAL | EXTERNAL |
|---|---|
| **Sales team** | Advisors |
| **Executives** | Service Partners |
| **Personalities** | Integration Partners |
| **Product team** | Content Creators |
| **Success team** | Influencers |

This carefully curated chorus of evangelists singing your story harmoniously is far more powerful than any solo performance.

Each individual brings unique proximity, credibility, perspective, and level of trust with your audience. Once you have this robust list, you can start evaluating and prioritizing who to activate.

## Step 2: Evaluate

When you first start identifying your potential evangelists, the list can seem daunting and overwhelming. How will you get all these influential people and organizations to collaborate? And how can you be sure they have relationships with the market you're trying to live in?

Now that you've cast a wide net with your list, it's time to niche down. Look for evangelists and partnerships where there is some level of reciprocity, and a personal relationship already exists. Jeff Bezos will likely be out of reach, so prioritize individuals within a company you have an existing connection with before pursuing broader partnerships.

You need to "map and tap": map out your evangelists and how they are situated around your buyers, and then document how you can tap into their influence. For example, can your marketing activities pull them in, include them, create with them, distribute through them, call back to them, highlight them, etc.?

Isaac and Logan leverage nearbound platforms like Reveal and audience research platforms like SparkToro to analyze important compatibility factors:

First, look at the audience and account overlap. Who shares the highest percentage of customers and prospects with you? A tool like Reveal gives you a 360° view of not just account overlaps, but also all the partners in that ecosystem that you could tap to support your objectives. SparkToro lets you see who shares the highest percentage of customers and prospects with you by analyzing social profiles and domains. Relevance is critical.

Next, evaluate positioning and narrative alignment. Do you share a similar point of view on market trends and the "promised land"? Assess complementarity on both product and story levels. It's not just about the product, but also about a complementary narrative.

Also, consider examining complementary abilities and reach. What unique strengths does each party bring to the table? Where can you fill gaps or amplify impact for each other? By combining strengths, you can deliver better content to a wider audience. Uncover these potential win-win situations and bring the best of each party to the table.

> **Pro tip**: When engaging with evangelists who have strong voices and followings, it's important to recognize that commenting on your posts or sharing them has an opportunity cost. Influencers on social media spend a significant amount of time "crediting" their audience with ungated, free advice, tips, tricks, and thought-provoking content. We refer to this as "social capital" throughout the book.
>
> The best approach to nearbound marketing in this context is to provide them with valuable content that aligns with their previous successful posts. Take 3-5 of their top posts and draft messages that complement their style and voice.
>
> Consider their style—whether it's choppy and to the point, or if they prefer storytelling with vivid details. Evangelists are unlikely to share content that doesn't fit their style, and asking them to write it from scratch may be burdensome. Keep in mind that this is an advanced strategy that can be highly effective, but it's important to strike the right balance. Feel free to reach out to me, Isaac Morehouse, or Logan Lyles on LinkedIn for more details on how to master social influence in the nearbound approach.

For example, you may have evangelists who are stronger in one area while you are stronger in another: video, events, owned media (such as newsletters or podcasts), product usage, or deep service work on big accounts. Leverage tangential and complementary strengths to create new capabilities, messages, reach, and influence. Additionally, assess the reach and willingness of potential evangelists to engage in personal activity on social media. This is a key requirement for activating personal brands as evangelists. Take note of individuals who are already active on social media and passionate about industry conversations, and for the big names, make it easy for them to share.

With these compatibility factors analyzed, you're ready to start collaborating.

If you want to take a smaller, incremental step, you can try an experiment in what Isaac and others call "permissionless marketing." This approach comes before over-planning or making big requests of an evangelist whom you're not sure will deliver. Start by subtly engaging the partner through social media shoutouts, sharing their content, and inviting them onto your podcast. This gives them the opportunity to reciprocate. When done well, this isn't something that you use against them for a future request. Instead, it's organic, and they naturally start doing more with you.

These small, low-pressure tests allow you to build trust gradually and get a feel for genuine compatibility before formalizing any partnership. Just as in the world of dating, you start by chatting to see if there is compatibility before jumping into a serious commitment. Meanwhile, you are monitoring their eagerness and receptivity to reciprocate and co-promote. These early interactions are an evaluation mechanism to identify ideal allies worth activating at scale. First impressions make a difference, control your first impressions where your value is seen.

## Step 3: Activate!

Once you've identified your top evangelists through careful evaluation, it's time to activate them. But first, clearly outline expectations and incentives. Will this be an informal partnership, or are you open to a paid sponsorship model? How are you tracking activity and performance and sharing that context with your own internal sellers, success teams, or partner teams? What about theirs?

Regardless of the level of formality, reciprocity is key. Ensure both parties understand the mutual benefits. You need a win-win partnership to activate surround sound marketing.

Once expectations are aligned, kick off a cadence of co-creation. You should establish a rhythm for how you work together. Who does what, by when? What is your weekly, monthly, and/or quarterly schedule for working together? When do you reflect on past experiences to learn from them, and when do you plan for the future?

For instance, if you're scheduling a podcast, don't just schedule the episode, post, and then ghost. Use the prep call to create snippets to promote its release for both parties. You should also create video snippets or highlights of the guests' best moments that make them look great and increase their social capital for sharing with their audience. Don't just ask them to share when published, bake into the cadence the expectation that you'll be giving them something to share that makes them look good. Done right, you'll be able to get promotion of the episode to be released and then promo once it's dropped if that's baked into your cadence and rituals for your partners.

Will Taylor, the Head of Partnerships at nearbound.com, does this weekly, monthly, and quarterly, and we've seen some of our biggest growth by adopting activation plays that span a regular cadence with the partner. He works with our internal social media and video teams to orchestrate our business rhythm with his partners, and they love him for it. Leslie Douglas, who leads Sales Programming & Thought Leadership for JB Sales (one of the largest sales communities in B2B), said it better than I ever could:

> **Leslie Douglas** · 8:12 AM
> Hey Jared! Will made it so easy and it was such an awesome conversation.

Making it easy is always the key.

As an interviewer, it's important to adopt a journalistic mindset. Local news reporters always have an abundance of content, even with their daily deadlines. They succeed by actively seeking out the action and connecting with the people involved in current events. Just as bystanders are eager to talk with reporters for a chance to be featured on the evening news, industry insiders are flattered to be asked for their views on trends in their area of expertise.

This journalistic approach grants you access to more influential voices, in service of your strategic narrative. Though you remain a marketer, your job is to stay focused on these strategic narratives, not to ask for endorsements. Their job is to provide an authentic perspective, not praise for your product. Ask them thoughtful questions that elicit your allies' organic perspectives on relevant industry issues and trends.

Then, you can repurpose the most engaging clips into micro content—seeding your social channels with authentic content straight from these influential voices. Track how these clips perform across platforms to refine your messaging and positioning based on what appears to resonate most with your audience.

## Step 4: Distribute—Make Them Famous

The fourth step of activating your evangelists is getting the word about your strategic narrative out to the people who need to hear it: your Ideal Customer Profile.

Remember that your task is to distribute *with* partners and evangelists, not through them.

Don't confuse partners and evangelists with channels of old, where the partner's job was to distribute your product. In nearbound marketing, partners are centers of gravity and proximity of trust, not pathways of transactions. To establish and maintain trust with your evangelists, you need to be able to go to the market and say, "You can trust us together."

Here, the aim should be to **make your partners famous first**. By portraying them in a positive light as the experts in their domain, you are providing them with an asset that they will want to share with their audience—your potential customers.

Today, you don't need to be a journalist at a major media company to make your partners famous. Anyone can establish themselves as a trusted content creator and get the message out using the tools of modern media.

You might be thinking, "Start another podcast? Isn't everyone and their grandma podcasting these days? How will I get heard among the noise?"

Don't expect the primary value of your podcast or LinkedIn account to come from immediate wide reach. When we started the Nearbound Podcast, we had zero audience. But then we started sharing clips and starting conversations around these snippets of wisdom from influencers in the partnerships ecosystem, and soon the signal began to get amplified organically.

After six months, we had created roughly 25 episodes with barely a couple thousand downloads. In a year, we had done ~50 episodes with a couple thousand more downloads—nothing to brag about. The real value wasn't in these numbers but in the trust built through the conversations themselves, plus the continuing conversations on LinkedIn about the truth bombs my evangelists were dropping on listeners that backed up our strategic narrative about the partnerships moment and what would eventually become nearbound. It didn't seem like a great idea at first (and some people told me so), but over 150 episodes in and at tens of thousands of downloads, you can see what happens when you get the right message to the right people, and *through* the right people at the right time.

B2B SaaS is still a world of small worlds, relatively speaking. Though a niche often looks crowded, you don't have to be the center of the universe to attract some of the brightest stars in your solar system. The winners are those who amplify the importance of existing stars and make them shine even brighter.

## Step 5: Understand

Colleagues who are stuck in the Digital Automation Era will likely want some assurance that the new marketing spend is getting results. You may know in your bones that your partnerships are delivering, but which half are bringing in the most new deals?

Tracking results and understanding what is working well versus what is not is crucial for optimizing and improving your nearbound marketing approach over time.

Aim to gather both quantitative and qualitative details to get the full picture of what's resonating.

On the quantitative side, make sure to leverage existing marketing tools already in place to monitor content performance. Although trust and influence are more valuable than data alone in the Nearbound Era, we are certainly not advocating discarding data completely. Just like when data replaced oil as the engine of business, we didn't stop using oil, we just valued it differently and tried to use it more efficiently and make the process less polluting.

Inserting UTM tracking codes into links shared by your evangelists is an obvious starting place, so you can see which content is driving traffic to landing pages, offers, and livestream sign-ups. Logan's team uses Shield to analyze and aggregate the organic social engagement of our evangelists on LinkedIn. Shield allows you to understand which posts are resonating the most based on total impressions, reach, and followers gained.

If you run LinkedIn thought leader ad campaigns to amplify your allies' content, be sure to tap into LinkedIn's Campaign Manager to monitor key metrics and performance. HockeyStack is a great tool for tracking attribution from LinkedIn ads. It models the entire customer journey across touchpoints and is phenomenal at tracking indirect downstream influence.

It's easy to get obsessed with quantifiable metrics when it comes to attribution. But if you want to truly embrace the Who Economy and nearbound, it helps to get comfortable layering some qualitative measures on top.

One of the best ways to find out who is influencing your buyer—partner or otherwise—is to *ask* and *listen*. There are a few powerful ways to do this.

Tools like Gong allow you to tap into sales call recordings and set up custom trackers. Configure these trackers to flag whenever your evangelists are mentioned by prospects.

One of the best qualitative reporting mechanisms is a free text box where prospects can provide an open-ended answer about how they heard about you. Chris Walker of Refine Labs refers to this as "self-reported attribution," which is a game changer for understanding how customers themselves answer questions such as, "Who referred you to us?" or, "How did you find out about us?"

When implementing the open-text field in Reveal forms and conversion points, we found exactly what Walker found with his clients: More than 50% of people mention a specific person or company. The surprising part is that analytics platforms completely overlook this aspect. To address this, we manually append the results to our conversions and record the contact and account information every month. This strategy is perhaps the perfect example of nearbound marketing in the Nearbound Era: you can get the data but the trust is what matters most. It's not "how" your tech stack says your buyers came to you, it's "who" those buyers say influenced them.

The self-reported attribution tactic is a blend of both.

We have conducted events with partners, and while the UTM links showed only slight increases in leads, signups, and demos, analyzing the call recordings and free-form text responses over the next 30 days revealed that as many as 50% mentioned the event. If we had relied solely on traditional marketing attribution, none of this would have been known to us.

Of course, these forms aren't always perfectly accurate. Nothing in the modern attribution stack is. Some responders may leave them blank or fill them with nonsense characters to proceed to the next page. However, they often capture a signal that the rigid dropdown forms overlook, providing you with the ammunition you need to demonstrate the impact of nearbound marketing. And let's be real—who would you trust more? What people actually say influenced them or what your operating model interprets?

Using your account mapping tool, you can also take a snapshot of the status of all the accounts that have partners attached at the beginning of each month, then again at the end of the month if you've run some kind of campaign with that partner and see which of those accounts moved from one stage to the next. This is not a perfect way to attribute influence, but it at least provides a starting point and prompts further investigation into the real journey of your customer and the real people involved.

Finally, set up #nearbound Slack or Teams channels for your internal and external evangelists to provide abundant anecdotal intel. You can encourage them to celebrate wins, screenshot particular comments and social proof, keep everyone updated, and note what content and topics spark discussion. As you both share wins, make sure you capture them for the quarterly report to your leadership on how nearbound marketing is working through a team of activated evangelists.

Do this, and you won't just have the data on your side, you'll also have an army of proof— people saying what's resonating and what's not, and then them calling out in your forms what was the thing that brought them over to you.

## Phase 5: Iterate and Expand

Once you achieve some initial success activating your first small group of evangelists, it's time to iterate and expand the program.

Here, it is important to avoid expanding too quickly. Resist the temptation to activate all potential evangelists at once. This can strain resources and disappoint early partners. Instead, start with a few proven success stories and gradually build momentum to improve the end marketing results.

Start by reviewing the results of your tracking key performance indicators (KPIs), both quantitative and qualitative. Look for what resonates in terms of content types, channels, and messaging. Additionally, gather direct feedback from your evangelists on what they find effective. Remember that their critiques or frustrations can be just as valuable as positive feedback on what is working, as iron sharpens iron.

With these insights, you will want to focus on amplifying what's working, whether it's specific partnerships, content formats, or distribution strategies. At the same time, make adjustments where efforts aren't paying off. The biggest wins will be your most effective recruiting mechanism for other evangelists, both internally and externally.

Finally, there is a meta component to scaling your nearbound marketing—you must evangelize successful evangelism. Use specific examples and results to showcase the value and attract new allies. When it works, it's your job to make people see it, get excited, and buy-in. Share how a LinkedIn post, interview, or podcast clip drove interest, higher metrics, or even better, new leads, in the #nearbound chat channels. Each time you do, you generate social proof—inviting the skeptics to the bandwagon.

Early wins spawn further investment and expansion. This will allow you to better execute the overlay of nearbound marketing onto all GTM teams, not just a siloed underlay within your marketing team. The more other teams see that it's working, the more they will raise their hands to pull the activation levers it creates—and the more your nearbound marketing machine will become self-perpetuating.

## ICE on the ABM

Remember, partnerships should not just be a department, but a strategy across *every* department. As mentioned at the outset of this section, the overlay model allows us to add partnerships and collaborative efforts *on top of* our existing work, rather than completely restructuring the systems we have already developed.

I find nearbound marketing attractive because it doesn't require a complete overhaul. Instead of destroying and rebuilding, nearbound motions can be integrated into every aspect of marketing, especially with a solid B2B foundation.

Perhaps the best way to demonstrate the power of acting with partnerships as an overlay is with Account Based Marketing (ABM).

Marketers are already aware of the surge in popularity of ABM, if not as an industry, at least as a fundamental practice. ABM marked a significant advancement for a large portion of B2B, as Sangram Vajre's rallying cry to "flip the funnel" became widespread in B2B marketing.

ABM focuses marketing and sales efforts on a defined list of targeted accounts rather than general activities aimed at a wider, or often undefined, audience. It recognizes that no method alone can reach, inspire, or influence the target audience. Trying to market broadly wastes resources on mismatches across the board. While ABM was not a panacea for all that ailed B2B before it, it moved the conversation in the right direction. Instead of focusing on **us**, it forced marketers to focus on **them**. The actual boss and center of the universe in B2B is the customer. Enumerating and naming them is powerful—both in what it reveals about how well you know your market and in how capable you are of meeting them where they are.

I remember the day when Allison Munro first crystallized the epiphany that "nearbound marketing is the next evolution of ABM."

In a LinkedIn post she explained how nearbound marketing transcends traditional ABM by integrating the collective strength of partners and ecosystem, transforming the way we engage with our target accounts.

# SURROUND SOUND MARKETING IN 5 PHASES

**Allison Munro** · 2nd
Chief Marketing & Ecosystem Officer @ Vena
8mo

Nearbound marketing is the next evolution of ABM.

That goes beyond your direct sellers to now include the sellers and marketers within your partners and ecosystem.

The simplest reason? Cold outbound is hard, interruptive and inefficient.

By focusing on account based engagement , we put our efforts towards helping the right fit accounts become aware of Vena Solutions (i.e., target).

And then prioritize the accounts who are demonstrating that they're in the market for a solution like ours (i.e., intent / problem identification).

Then we further engage new accounts early and often while also engaging people from accounts who have come to know us (i.e., trust).

We then focus our sales teams' efforts on these accounts (i.e., timing), which creates a better experience that's more relevant for our buyers, sellers and partners, while driving repeatability and efficiency.

Now introduce your partners and the accounts that know and trust your partners. And the accounts your direct sales teams and partners have in common or overlap.

Combining the power of target, trust, intent, and timing extends to these partners — helping identify the accounts we have in common, focusing our sales efforts in a co-sell and co-serve motion.

That creates more value and a higher likelihood of finding the perfect match.

How are you preparing for the next generation of ABM? I'd love to hear your thoughts.

#Marketing #ABM #Sales

39                                                              11 comments

Munro articulated a pivotal shift: moving away from the traditional, laborious cold outbound tactics to a more nuanced, account-based engagement strategy. This approach, which focuses on identifying and prioritizing accounts that align with your company's offerings and demonstrate a clear market need, emphasizes the critical importance of a well-defined Ideal Customer Profile (ICP). This method doesn't rely on guesswork for potential interest, but instead targets those who have already shown they are in the market for a product like yours.

Carefully researching your Ideal Customer Profile allows you to identify the accounts with the highest potential fit. Again, this is marketing 101—nothing special so far. However, ABM often stops there. Once you have targeted your ideal accounts, how do you actually reach them? This is where the nearbound approach shines.

As mentioned in Chapter 2, Mark Kilens, Isaac Morehouse, and I created a simple framework for overlaying nearbound to any motion. We call it ICE:

1. Identify
2. Collaborate
3. Execute

ICE makes ABM easy. This framework is intentionally direct and uncomplicated, designed to overlay nearbound strategies into existing marketing frameworks, regardless of their complexity or scale.

**Identify**: Determine who the target accounts trust and their locations within existing networks. Layer in nearbound data into your target account list. Identify accounts with partner overlap and the specific partners involved.

**Collaborate**: Engage with relevant partners to develop a strategy for reaching the accounts. Prioritize collaboration based on the gravity and proximity of the partners to maximize network effects and exponential reach inherent to any ecosystem.

**Execute**: Run the plays and measure the impact of the activities based on the attention, pipeline, and revenue it drives against those actual accounts.

Marketing can serve as so much more than a lead-feeder to sales. With nearbound, marketing teams can surround the market with influence and home in on target accounts with partners. Marketers don't need to be the loudest voice to reach customers if they are partnering with the most trusted voice.

In the next section, we'll show you a proven method for sales teams to close more deals using the three-fold play of nearbound intel, influence, and intros.

# Part 3
## Nearbound Sales

> *"'Your network equals your net-worth' is more than a cute quote— it's a necessity for businesses. Sellers need to get strategic about the relationships they have. The world of cold calls and emails has an expiration date, and the only way to prepare for it is by nurturing trust in your ecosystem. Today, the fundamental nature of sales focuses on relationships, adaptation, and, ultimately, delivering value to the people we aim to serve. If you're not evolving towards this goal, you'll be out of a job. And soon."*
>
> —Scott Leese, Founder & CEO of Scott Leese Consulting

## CHAPTER 6

# HOW SELLING REALLY WORKS

My phone vibrated again. I looked at the number.

This was attempt number four. Same salesperson, same number. In a consecutive four-minute timeline.

If you work in sales, you've heard of what is jokingly referred to as the "triple-tap"—reaching out to a prospect through three separate channels in a short span of time, or calling not just twice when someone doesn't answer, but three times consecutively.

But four times?! Do we call this the "quad call?" And why stop there?

If four attempts to reach me via cold call didn't work, why not five, six, or seven?

I'll never know how many more times the persistent rep tried to reach out to me with his crucial message, because I blocked the number after the fourth call.

The phone is not dead. But awfully cold, as in, *"I'd never interact with your brand at all,"* cold. It cannot possibly recover from this trend to its former heights. You have to earn the right to get a call with me now, and millions more join that group monthly. We're not holier than thou, we just can't possibly allow dozens of calls to interrupt the day before lunch. For better or worse, bad actors ruined cold calling.

It's not just our phones that are getting flooded with outbound. Buyers are bombarded at every turn with the same tired tactics as sales representatives become increasingly cute and AI creates exponentially more content to meet their quotas.

You might be thinking these are strategies. They aren't. Tactics like this are just farts in the wind. Whether or not someone can smell them that day, they still stink.

The email with, "my boss asked me to call you," also stinks. Starting off a relationship with deception is a surefire way to destroy your ability to influence potential buyers. If your C-suite wanted to talk to me, they'd email me, not you. If you're a buyer, you know this is true.

In fact, I recently heard a Senior VP Sales of a $1B company ask their entire executive team a question that woke everyone up.

"Let's assume that the team hits 100% of all their outbound sales activity targets across 100% of reps," he asked. In other words, not a single rep missed a single outbound activity target, AE or SDR. He continued, "Even if that were the case, does anyone here honestly believe that will get the company to our pipeline or sales targets we've set?"

Everyone in that room was shaking their heads. But not up and down. They were shaking them from left to right.

Aaron Ross's excellent book *Predictable Revenue* changed SaaS sales forever. Except, now, it's *unpredictable*.

This same VP went on to describe to me how they used to be an inbox zero person, but now have even given up—not only on clearing out the 7-10 outbound emails they receive every hour, but even on answering internal emails from their team members.

"How is anyone ever going to sell me cold if I can't even reply to internal emails because we're so overwhelmed?" he asked in exasperation.

Here's the reality: in addition to being a VP of Sales for a major SaaS company, the man I was talking to is also a buyer. Probably not unlike so many of you reading this today.

He was asking his execs this pessimistic question because he had completely lost faith in the old predictable revenue model. Even if all the activity targets were maxed and hit and done well, they had no shot at ever seeing themselves in their buyer's shoes anymore and hence making the number.

I don't want to fully out his former employer (or mine!), but his name is Kyle. And Kyle is someone I've worked with across a couple of different companies. He's never been "partner-led," or an "ecosystem evangelist," he's just a widely respected sales leader by his colleagues with his fingerprints on dozens of millions in sales and hundreds of sellers.

Before we ended our chat, Kyle said something interesting:

"After I decided to give up (almost) entirely on my inbox, I had one of my friends text me and bring up someone who was trying to meet with me. He said I'd probably get sold to, but that the person was honest and good to know either way, and I should take a meeting. So I did. That is the only way sales are going to get done today—through contacts I know and trust."

Bingo.

That's nearbound sales in a nutshell. If you take away nothing else from this chapter, takeaway Kyle's statement: it's about threading the right people into your sales process, not just changing your script or your sales pitch. Once again, it's about *who*, not *how*.

By now, you're probably tired of hearing the same variation on the same basic point made from so many different angles. "I get it," you might be thinking, "Inbound and outbound are getting harder. The tactics that defined those eras don't work the same anymore because of the rise in noise and the decline in trust."

But the point isn't to declare the old playbooks dead. Nearbound is not about ending outbound or inbound. I think *we all* would have loved for inbound to end outbound. No, seriously, I mean it. What salesperson would NOT prefer a demo request assignment over a cold call activity? But that didn't happen.

Instead of killing outbound, inbound augmented outbound. Inbound and the marketing automation revolution diversified our revenue mix and brought more plays to the repertoire of sellers for building and accelerating pipeline. Not every call had to be cold. Yes, the potential buyer might not be expecting your call, but calling someone who had at least downloaded your company's eBook or attended your webinar was far better than them having zero context for the brand you were calling about.

Nearbound doesn't ask you to scrap inbound and outbound and reinvent the wheel. It amplifies inbound and outbound by adapting them to the moment we're in—a moment that is hungry for trust and connection.

This explains why some pioneers of nearbound sales tended to rise up during eras of outbound and inbound that proceeded our current moment.

Jill Rowley's sales origin story as a once-in-a-generation seller illustrates the immense power of nearbound sales long before these motions had names. I've called Jill the "Queen of Social Selling," because, when it comes to the promised land, Jill's not only been there, but her greatest superpower is helping other people get there too. She became one of the top sales professionals and one of the most respected community voices of this era by surrounding customers with a web of trust—where she put it all on the line for her customers and community, time and again. And best of all, she has the receipts.

That's why I wanted Jill to share her story in her own words. It's worth paying attention to. Jill knows what she's talking about. Have you ever heard of an individual AE who was responsible for 40% of the revenue of a company with $100M+ in ARR?

Jill was.

For many of her hundreds of thousands of followers (myself included) I didn't even know this story or its full nearbound roots until recently. You wouldn't be reading this book were it not for Jill.

So, I'll politely excuse myself for the rest of this chapter and let Jill tell the story.

# How I Crushed Quota with the Power of Nearbound Sales

By Jill Rowley

"You continue to be the only person I've ever heard of who sold 40% of the revenue in the history of a company with more than $100M in ARR."

That was the general counsel at Eloqua. We had a good relationship, and he was blown away by the success I was having selling marketing automation into a market that barely knew what to do with it yet.

My success was not accidental. I had stumbled into something that, at the time, didn't have a name, process, or any tech to support and scale it. I stumbled into the power of *nearbound sales*.

Nearbound sales is about trust, influence, and value. It's about surrounding the buyer with the people who influence them—partners, analysts, subject matter experts, and people who have been where your buyers want to go.

## Selling at the Dawn of a New Era

At the time, the majority of CMOs were brand marketers doing PR. I was selling marketing automation software in a market where few knew what it was. Demand Generation was nascent and marketing ops wasn't yet a function.

A massive transformation was needed.

Here was this powerful technology that few knew how to implement, and had little incentive internally to do so. Marketing was measured on lead count; not quality.

## I Couldn't Do It Alone

One of my early customers in 2004 was the SVP of Marketing at Ellie Mae, Dave Lewis. Dave got it. He fought all the internal battles to get marketing automation in place. His persistence led them on a journey of transformation from old school to new school and they built modern, data-driven, automated programs that turned into pipeline and revenue.

We helped Dave become wildly successful. He reached the promised land. Meanwhile, most marketing teams were still doing "batch and blast" emails. They didn't know how to do things like lead nurturing, lead scoring, or multi-touch campaigns, and had no marketing ops to support them.

Dave saw tremendous potential in the marketing automation industry. He wanted to help more companies get started and do it right. He asked if I would partner with him. With zero hesitation, I said I was all in. Dave organized and led our local user group, he booked the room, ran the sessions, and even bought the bagels. When his agency was just getting started in 2007, Dave brought all but one thing to the table: leads.

I had a pipeline. I had customers who needed help. This is counterintuitive to most salespeople, but I decided the best thing to do was to **bring my leads to him.**

Dave had credibility, experience, results, and trust. I knew he could help me because he spoke my buyer's language and had walked in their shoes. He'd been to their promised land.

Connecting customers to a partner like this not only helps pre-sale, it helps get customers to value faster post-sale. Salespeople don't need to be altruists to care about customer success. Happy, successful customers are your best advocates.

Many of our most successful customers ended up working with Dave. And when it was time to land Salesforce as a customer (after a long history of partnering with them), guess who I brought in to co-sell with me?

Our data showed deals that included partners had higher conversion rates, higher velocity, higher win rates, better retention and expansion, and higher NPS.

### How I Won with Nearbound

I partnered with the right people at the right time. The buyer doesn't want to tell you about their business; they want you to know about their business. If you can get that insight and intel from someone who already has the trust, you're coming in ready.

I studied customer stories to find patterns. One year, we had 176 submissions for our annual customer awards. I printed and organized them in binders. I read every single one. It helped me identify our most successful customers and partners and allowed me to be a better matchmaker. If a potential customer wanted to do lead scoring, I'd match them to a partner that specialized in lead scoring. If a potential customer wanted to do multichannel campaigns, I'd match them to a partner that specialized in multichannel.

My job wasn't to sell. It was to facilitate a buying process. Doing it with partners was how I won deals and made customers more successful.

## What Does Nearbound Sales Mean for You?

There are two insights from my story directly relevant to today.

**First is the power of tapping into nearbound knowledge in the sales process**. I looked at every winner of our highly coveted annual awards and asked which partners they worked with. I got to know those partners well. In fact, in addition to employee and customer awards, we even created partner awards. I built relationships with all those winners too.

I knew that I didn't have everything my customers wanted. But if I could find who did and bring that to the table, I'd win more deals. It worked.

**Second is the fact that the same pattern that happened in marketing then is happening with sales now**. Most sales teams today are stuck in the past, just like most marketing teams were then. Few have any processes or technology in place to tap into the immense power of nearbound data hiding right next door, in their ecosystem.

## Nearbound Sales is a Superpower

I always made Presidents Club, won employee of the year, was on the NASDAQ when Eloqua IPO'd, and became a recognized leader in the industry all while being an individual quota 'caring' sales rep. I was doing nearbound sales.

You have an advantage I lacked. I was doing all of this identification and pattern matching manually. (Remember the 176 customer award submissions I mentioned?). Today, you've got powerful tools like Reveal and resources like nearbound.com at your disposal to accelerate your ability to tap into crucial information and build a nearbound sales motion that makes you money and the real boss happy—the customer.

That's why I'm so grateful for this book and for the rising movement, community, and industry around nearbound. Relying on outbound and inbound alone won't get you to your promised land and it won't get your customers to theirs.

In the Outbound Era, ABC meant "Always Be Closing." In the Nearbound Era, ABC means "Always Be Connecting."

Remember, your network is your net worth.

—Jill Rowley

# CHAPTER 7

# THE NEARBOUND SALES BLUEPRINT

Jill's story sets the stage for the timeless and increasingly important power of applying nearbound principles to sales. But it gets even better: this chapter is where the real action happens, where the blueprint is laid out for you to follow on your journey to achieve your goals.

The Nearbound Sales Blueprint is a dead simple way to operationalize plays from sellers that utilize partners in the revenue mix, without altering the structure of your organization or attempting to rebuild it from the ground up.

The Blueprint is comprised of three steps:

1. Nailing your nearbound sales math
2. Creating your nearbound account list
3. Running the 3 I's of nearbound sales - Intel, Influence, and Intros

Companies like Qualtrics and Box are not only using nearbound sales and the 3 I's, but they're also orienting their entire partner ecosystem around them to drive sales. Take a look at a newsletter they sent to all their partners:

> **box**
>
> ### July 2023 Box Partner Newsletter
>
> **WELCOME**
>
> **Hello Partners!**
>
> We want to let you know of our commitment to Nearbound selling, which is all about Partner alignment, inclusive of joint events, webinars, and overall collaborative business build. As we're ramping up more partner events, we know that as partners we are the source for mutual MQLs, SQLs and stronger pipeline. By using 360 mapping technology, we can better understand, not just who our customers are, but which partners they have and want to work with. As a Partner GTM team, we're focusing on targeting opportunity, mapping pursuit, and working with partners to win that business. In order to do this, there are 3 ways we want to align Nearbound tactics with you, our Partners:
> - Intelligence - We as partners have market and account insights, and can help each other understand our customers better, their tech landscape, and stay ahead of industry trends and RFPs.
> - Introductions - Nothing beats a warm introduction to a buyer, champion or decision maker/LOB leader, as well as potential customers and prospects. We want to facilitate introductions for each other that enable relationship building and ultimately joint pursuit of opportunity, so that we can close deals faster together than we do alone.
> - Influence - When our partner vouch for and recommend Box, we all win! Partner services, solutions, endorsements, case studies, and testimonials can significantly enhance Box credibility and reputation.

*Source: July 2023 Box Worldwide Partner Newsletter*

And you can too, more easily than you think.

# Step 1: Nailing your Nearbound Sales Math

**Goal:** Nail your nearbound sales math & calculate your optimal nearbound sales mix.

Sales leaders have a target revenue mix across different sales channels. Let's walk through a simple example:

Outbound and inbound drives most of your team's activities today. Maybe your current revenue mix is 50% outbound, 40% inbound, and 10% partner. But those channels alone aren't getting you to your targets. Even though your sellers spend most, if not all, of their time on outbound and inbound activities, those activities only make up 2/3 of your total sales productivity and pipeline.

| Outbound | Inbound | x? |

0% revenue                                100% revenue

By this point in our journey together, you are convinced that you need to get to a healthier mix. Given your win rates and average sales cycles when partners are involved, let's say you determine that your revenue mix should be ⅓ each for outbound, inbound, and nearbound.

How would you get there?

You haven't focused on optimizing this channel yet. As a result, you're leaving a lot of potential untapped.

Of course, you can't ditch outbound and inbound completely. But you can start to shift the dial by taking a portion of the activity that was going to those channels and dedicating it to high-potential nearbound partner accounts instead.

To hit this hypothetical, here's what it would entail:

- Around 1/3 of your open opportunities should include partner presence
- Around 1/3 of sales activities target nearbound partner plays
- Around 1/3 of accounts assigned to each seller have partners attached

The "partner attach rate" simply refers to the percentage of accounts, activities, or deals linked to partners. You can track this both at the individual rep level and company-wide.

This involves straightforward math, not magic. And putting it into practice is equally straightforward:

1. Determine how many accounts each rep owns per quarter (e.g. 100)
2. Ensure that 33 of those 100 accounts have partners attached for nearbound plays.
3. At the start of each quarter (or period when accounts are assigned), leadership, the partner manager, and the rep pick the

33 accounts with the most influential partner overlap to commit 33 of those accounts as nearbound accounts.

Those become your nearbound target account list—the sales equivalent of the nearbound ABM target account list we discussed in the Marketing Chapter. Just like the marketing team uses the ABM list to target the companies that best fit their niche or ICP (aka, the companies with the highest potential conversation) through the influence of the ecosystem to avoid wasted time and resources, the sales team uses the nearbound target account list to strategically tap into trust and influence from partners to surround and shorten their sales cycles, and to close more deals.

## Step 2: Creating your Nearbound Account List

**Goal:** Get strategic with partners to drive higher revenue and mutual benefit.

Now that you have high-level alignment on your company's goals, your individual KPIs, and how attach rates and activities can guide your maturity in determining your revenue mix, it's time to operationalize them. In our example, we said that each rep should have 33 accounts on their Nearbound account list.

### First: Sort the accounts with the most impactful partner overlap

The first task is to gather your team—typically the account executive, sales manager, and partner manager—to determine which accounts have the most partner overlap using some basic account mapping.

During this meeting, each member of the team has distinct roles and responsibilities. The account executive is responsible for planning, documenting, and preparing their plays based on the discussion. The sales manager takes on the role of a liaison, learning which partners are more or less effective over time, and holding their account executive accountable, while also holding the partner manager to the same standard.

Meanwhile, the partner manager helps to determine which partners have the best relationships and surfaces details such as when the prospect became a customer of a partner, the strength and willingness of a given partner, and the particular joint value proposition of each partner. They also receive and give feedback on previous nearbound sales plays run by this rep with these or other partners in the past to improve.

## Second: Identify which partners have the most relevant signals to run nearbound sales plays against

Next, you will be looking for signals in your chosen list to see which partners are the ripest with opportunity.

Perhaps two integration partners of yours closed your target account in the last three months. What business initiative(s) may have precipitated the possibility of these sales? Or, just as important, what business challenges were they solving? And for who? Just like Jill would, add these two integration partners to the partner pipeline, and include this account in the nearbound account list.

Or maybe a partner just renewed your customer. Ask them why. Perhaps a partner has an open opportunity to upsell a current client on another product or service. What prompted the further investment?

The main objective of this part of your meeting is to closely examine each partner relationship and identify the most relevant signals for gathering intelligence, influence, or potential introductions (the three "I's", which we'll get to soon). Once you determine the appropriate partner contact, ask how the Partner Manager on your team will initiate the conversation with an Account Executive, Customer Success, or Account Manager.

## Third: Identify the Relevant Relationships

Identify the personas involved in the account you're speaking with, as well as those that have relationships with key decision-makers. Focus on their roles or departments.

Often, sales teams run into roadblocks when the department they are targeting is not the one who makes the final decision about whether to buy—or even engage. For example, the AE might be speaking with the Demand Generation team at a prospective company. The rep sends information and tries to schedule meetings. But the Demand Gen folks keep postponing and making excuses. They say things like "Sorry, we're too swamped right now to explore this."

It turns out, the marketing operations team actually controls the budget and technology choices. So, Demand Gen can't move forward without the green light from marketing ops.

Marketing ops may be hesitant to engage for a few reasons:

- They are busy with other initiatives
- They already have solutions in place and don't want to rock the boat
- They don't know or trust the seller who is reaching out

This is where partnerships become so valuable. They provide a foot in the door. Using an account mapping tool, a seller might see that one of their partners recently closed deals with the VP of marketing ops and marketing ops Manager at this prospect company.

This means the marketing ops team already knows and likes working with that partner, and that the team is very likely working on implementing the solution they just bought. So, instead of trying to push through the Demand Gen roadblock, the seller can work with their partner for an introduction to marketing ops. The trust the partner has can transfer to the seller, and marketing ops will be much more open to engaging if the outreach comes from a familiar, trusted source.

In this scenario, it's much wiser to get the answers to the test, or "intel", from your partner on why there is a disconnect in your approach. Use your partner to influence their contacts to take your solution evaluation seriously, and to schedule that meeting they have been postponing.

Repeat this process until you have identified the personas for all of the 33 accounts and the same number (or more) of partners with whom you can collaborate to drive and accelerate pipeline growth faster than outbound or inbound efforts alone. We recommend doing this monthly or quarterly, depending on how often account books refresh and how frequently partner relationships change. And, of course, these views of partner overlap are easily surfaced in things like seller day-in-the-life reports and dashboards, as well as pipeline and forecast views via HubSpot, Salesforce, or your favorite CRM for reinforcement.

Establish an actionable, measurable, and repeatable A-to-Z process that overlays against your current sales motion without reinventing it. Both partnership and sales teams can execute this process to implement nearbound sales plays and drive revenue.

Building a nearbound account list with 33 accounts out of your 100 is table stakes if you need to drive 1/3rd of your revenue with partners—what I call "proactive nearbound." But it doesn't have to stop there. Funnels and prospects are constantly in motion, as are partner relationships. You may create a list of nearbound accounts, but a week later, a friendly and helpful partner may close one of those accounts, giving you a new signal to tap into—or "reactive nearbound." Work with tools that provide an intelligent and proactive way to overlay nearbound to any sales process that has assigned accounts. But don't forget to take advantage of these signals as they happen in real-time.

Technology like Reveal and similar tools make this possible to execute with up-to-date second-party data—reactive in the ways that matter and signals that live where you are. This makes it possible to automatically send important partnership data to sellers when certain events occur—events such as when:

- A seller gets assigned a new account with a high partner signal
- A partner relationship changes with one of the rep's accounts

For example, if a tech or service partner renews, upsells, closes, or opens an opportunity with an owned account, you can customize notifications via triggers to email or Slack the account team. The notification contains all the relevant details about the partnership event. And best of all, it goes right into the seller's CRM field of view in HubSpot or Salesforce too. Sales managers, partner teams, and/or revenue operations can customize these automatic notifications, and choose which accounts or partners trigger a notification and when it is sent. You can also track any follow-up the rep does related to the notification. This ensures the CRM has complete data on partnerships that influenced deals.

In short, the technology handles monitoring partnerships and routing important events to the right sellers, making it easy for them to capitalize on partnerships. This is the kind of manual tracking work that Jill Rowley had to spend hours on each week. Now, the information is at your fingertips without even having to think about it.

## Making the Data Work for You

The data from a nearbound revenue platform can also drive automatic tasks to help sellers capitalize on partnerships.

Some examples:

- **When a prospect is already a customer of a partner**, you can trigger an automated email sequence. The emails educate the prospect on how the rep's solution complements the partner's.
- **When an open deal is an open deal of your partner(s)**, you can create a task for an AE to reach out to the partners to strategize a co-selling opportunity.
- **When a cold lead is a customer of a partner,** you can automatically send a Slack message to an SDR. The message lists relevant partners who may provide introductions or intelligence.

These automated triggers integrate partnerships into the sales workflow from the start. They help reps react when it matters most to pursue partnership opportunities. The key is using new networked databases through a nearbound revenue platform to your CRM and sales tools. This doesn't replace your sales manager or partner managers or CRMs—it simply amplifies their hard work to create joint success across all of your teams.

Daily, weekly, and monthly operations demonstrate that partnerships are not merely confined to a single department. Rather, they are a strategic element that should be integrated across all departments and phases of the customer journey. The partnerships team cannot utilize software like Reveal in isolation. They must collaborate with the sales and marketing teams to break down organizational barriers and unlock their true value. This is how nearbound account lists are created and brought to life, where nearbound sales plays rule the day. (*We'll get into this more in the chapter on the Rhythm of Nearbound*).

## Step 3: Running the Nearbound Sales Plays

**Goal:** Master the 3 I's of nearbound sales (Intel, Influence, and Intros) to accelerate your pipeline by leveraging your partners' trust and access.

Once you have decided who to target first and who will help you get your foot in the door, it's time to pick the play best suited to your goals.

But first, a warning:

Based on the data of over 12,000 companies on the Reveal network as of early 2024, running nearbound sales plays with partner attach in aggregate results in:

- Increasing the number of open opportunities by 33%
- Increasing win rates by 41% or
- Reducing time to close by 43%
- Decreasing your CAC
- Increasing productivity per rep

There are three primary plays that power this playbook. We call them "The 3 I's of Nearbound Sales":

1. Intel
2. Influence
3. Intro

To the newcomer, the three I's look like cheat codes that unlock the game of sales on "easy mode." For nearbound pioneers like Jill Rowley, these plays have been standard operating procedure since the early 2000s.

Let's start with Intel.

# 1. Intel

Intel refers to any information your partners and/or partnership technology can provide you about an opportunity. Examples of intel include:

- The best point of contact in your prospect's company, including champions, decision-makers, and even blockers.
- The technology the prospect is currently using. (Integrations with existing tech are a top priority for 76% of buyers, according to E&Y).
- The prospect's top pain points and how they articulate them. Remember, buyers are more likely to engage with brands that use language similar to their own.
- New initiatives and goals in the prospect's organization. If they are pivoting, it's because they either have a problem that's causing them to do so, or they see an opportunity they want to pursue. How can you help them achieve their objectives?

When it comes to accelerating your pipeline, intel is the gas pedal.

Every time you schedule a call or a meeting, the person on the other end of the line or sitting across the table, will be expecting you to have done your homework and present a clear direction—both for the meeting itself and, ideally, in the follow-up actions the meeting catalyzes.

Intel is how you as a seller can get "the answers to the test."

Why spend the first half of the call groping for those answers when this trusted information has already been earned by your partner?

Intel is information that they aren't advertising to just anyone. Obtaining this information helps you position yourself and your strategy alongside the companies with which your prospect has established relationships.

## How to Get Quality Intel

Now that you know what intel you need and why it's important, let's break down how to get it:

**Use what you know**: Analyze your data from a tool like Reveal to find partner presence. Leverage the relationship you have with your partner and what you know about them to draft a value proposition.

For instance, let's say your partner has a solution, and you know the main problems that their audience faces, how can you create messages that explain how your solution improves the procedures that the audience already has with your partner's technology?

**Help first:** You might not yet have the intel you need on a prospect, but you might know that the prospect is a long-time customer of your partner. You also know that one of your customers is a prospect of that same partner. Reach out to the partner with valuable intel on the account they're going after. Help them, then ask for what you need.

This plays on the innate human tendency to reciprocate favors. Don't do this in a manipulative way or treat the partner like they "owe you one." Just trust that by scratching their back, they'll be more inclined to scratch yours when the time comes.

**Pull from the collective knowledge**: To get a better understanding of what a customer wants and needs, don't just rely on one partner's information. Use the tools at your disposal to see all the partners that have a relationship with that customer. Gather intel from each partner you have a good relationship with to get a holistic view of the customer's goals and pain points.

At the end of the day, you must reach out to the partner. An email or direct message is usually most appropriate.

The partner manager is responsible for delivering the message to the appropriate person on the partner's team, whether it be a fellow AE or someone from the customer success department. The AE's role is to ensure that the outreach is as clear and actionable as possible.

Here's an "Intel" email template you can steal right now:

> "Hey [Partner name X],
>
> I'm talking to [contact Y] next week over at [account Z]. I noticed you closed them last quarter with buy-in from the [A department].
>
> So that I'm presenting the most relevant case about our [joint value proposition of B], would you be willing to share any intel about the business initiative you aligned to?
>
> A few of your top bullets would be extremely helpful.
>
> Respectfully,
>
> [Rep name]
>
> P.S. Or if you're open to hopping on a call for 15 minutes, maybe I could offer up some intel from my side on the [C account(s)] you're selling to. I owned these opportunities and would be happy to trade notes."

The "intel play" can provide valuable insights at any point in a sales cycle, helping to build or accelerate pipeline momentum.

Let me give an example that really opened one seller's eyes. This guy was perhaps the most anti-partnerships rep I've ever met, once telling me, **"Partnerships are a way for marketing to take credit for my own pipeline and deals."**

His partner-pill moment finally arrived when he figured out how simple yet powerful the intel play could be.

Many B2B deals involve procurement—the department that makes final purchasing decisions. Procurement focuses on getting the best terms and pricing. They can be tough negotiators. So, this seller made it his mission to get intelligence on how procurement operated at his largest, most complex prospects. He worked with partners who already sold to those accounts successfully. He asked the partners to share their insights on procurement's processes and expectations. Armed with this inside intel from partners, the rep was able to tailor his pitches. He addressed procurement's needs upfront.

The results spoke for themselves. The rep achieved the highest win rate among enterprise-level deals. He also booked bigger ACV deals, too.

He never would have had this success going in blind. The intel from partners gave him the inside track. Funny, it's as if having the answers to the test before you take it gives you a shot at a higher score.

## 2. Influence

Influence is crucial in the new era of B2B sales—it's both everywhere and at the center of the Who Economy. Buyers are tuned out to traditional outreach methods. They instead turn to trusted advisors in their network for guidance.

As Jay McBain notes, the typical B2B buyer has around 28 "moments" before choosing a vendor. These are key interactions, events, or touchpoints in their buying journey.

Only 4 of those 28 moments might involve direct communication with potential vendors. The other 24 moments are driven by external influences, like peer recommendations, consultant advice, or industry chatter. Vendors need to tap into this world of influence beyond their direct reach.

Picture each buyer as being surrounded by a "gravitational field" of other companies and advisors. Their opinions and relationships exert a pull on the buyer's decision-making.

The strongest "gravity" comes from those closest to the buyer. For example, an implementation consultant who works closely with the company will have more sway than a casual conference connection. This is where partnerships become so valuable. Partners have already established trusted bonds with buyers. Their influence flows naturally, without raising the buyer's sales radar.

With nearbound, vendors can surround buyers with gentle influence from multiple trusted partners. This expands their gravitational field and pull. By surrounding your prospects with influence from their trusted service providers and community members, your organization can see that the hypothetical 33% goal for attach rate turns into more than 33% of revenue.

Here's an "Influence" email template you can steal right now:

> "Hey [Partner Contact Name - AM], I'm talking to [Opportunity Contact] over at [Opportunity Account] next week.
>
> I noticed [they just renewed with you] last quarter. They mentioned in their last call how important [Company Name] was to [their strategy].
>
> A part of the success plan I put together for them next week is our [integration]. This is my first time talking with their [Contact Title] and I wanted to see if you'd be able to put in a good word with [Contact Name] about our partnership and the [integration] over email or a call prior to then?
>
> If so, I put together an email below that you can use that should highlight our joint value proposition.
>
> Take a look and if you don't mind sending it over, will you let me know?
>
> In partnership,
>
> [Seller Name]
>
> [Email to be forwarded copy]
>
> P.S. It looks like you share a couple of accounts with upsell opportunities that I recently sold as well like [Account Name 1 & 2]. Happy to discuss or help there if that's valuable, just lmk."

If you're a seller, you can leverage this template right now, today, on your nearbound account list. It's not quite a referral, it's not quite outbound, and it's certainly not channel.

**It's nearbound.** It takes advantage of the trust and credibility the partner already enjoys. And it's far more effective than a seller trying to push the merits directly.

As Jill Rowley likes to remind sellers, you have to "Show me you know me." The corollary to this saying is to show buyers you care about them by integrating partners buyers already rely on. This is the power of carefully orchestrated influence.

There are dozens of permutations of similar templates or scenarios that you can use, develop, or tweak. Of course, it takes some preparation and practice to get these messages in front of the right partner contacts and influence the right account contacts. However, the effort involved is no greater than that of sending personalized and well-researched outbound emails.

Which would you rather work on: the one with a 1 in 100 chance or the one with a 1 in 3 chance? Like everything in this chapter, the math is simple. As a seller, your choice should be simple, too.

AEs were not elected as Supreme Ruler over your accounts; you were assigned to them, they were not assigned to you. Instead of exercising some kind of inherited authority, you exercise influence, which must be earned.

Charlene Li, an Executive Transformation Coach and the author of *Disruption Mindset*, defines power as influence through three types:

1. **Referential power** is all about connection, and you build it by finding, identifying, and connecting with people in different areas.
2. **Informational power** is achieved by sharing the information usually safeguarded by leadership with the entire organization.
3. **Expertise** focuses on identifying "people who have an area of expertise and work[ing] with them to develop that expertise…make sure they are tapping into informational and referential power, too, so that they're able to expand their influence."

If you want to put the "Executive" back in Account Executive, it requires the competency and ability to translate referential, informational, and expert influence into plans and actions.

In other words, to be an "Executive," you must have the influence to help, the means to share information, and the experts who help you master and expand it.

Account executives work with and *manage* people who bring referential, informational, and expert influence to your accounts: partners, influencers, former customers, etc.

If you want to put the "Executive" back into Account Executive, start managing influence.

## 3. Intros

Introductions represent the holy grail of nearbound sales. Intros are the most valuable if obtained, but the most sophisticated to execute—and the riskiest if you screw it up.

Before we begin, let me make something abundantly clear: **the most surefire way to never get an intro is by only asking for a referral.** Referrals often involve asking contacts to mention your name, without providing the key context. For example, a referral may sound like: "You should check out my friend Jason's software company. He's a great guy."

An intro, on the other hand, sounds like this: "Jason's company helped solve the same problems we faced around XYZ. I think you'd find real value in their platform for C and D reasons."

See the difference? Intros require care, not just name-dropping.

By using the intro play, understand that you are attempting to leverage trust at its highest level with your partner as a seller.

Using the intro play means you are no longer the pesky, untrustworthy corporation filling up the prospect's inbox with automated emails. Instead, you are being ushered into the conversation by a community member that the prospect trusts. With the right introduction, your partner's trust will be transferred onto you, the seller.

But tread lightly. That trust is tentative. So, in the words of the CEO who taught me the most, David Cancel, "Don't F it up."

## "Don't F it Up"

When it comes to meaningful introductions, preparation is key. There is no winging it or relying on generic pitches. Instead, you need to have the intel to speak confidently about the ways you are going to make that prospect's operations better (this is why intel comes before intros in the three I's).

Here are some tips for getting the most out of the intro play and guaranteeing that you don't destroy the relationship with your partner before you ever get to leverage their trust with your prospect.

## Come Prepared

Before you even ask for the introduction, you should have your value proposition homed in. You need to know how your solution is going to improve the prospect's work and their company's success. There is no winging it. Make sure that you can speak confidently about the ways you are going to make their operations better.

## Be Ready to Help

The trust the partner has earned with the prospect is not something they will be willing to transfer to just anyone. You need to make it clear that you understand the value of your ask and be willing to reciprocate. If you can show that you care about their needs and their success, you will be more likely to get their support.

Nearbound sales provides an opportunity for the sales team to work closely with the Partner team on what they do best:

Help.

Partner teams can focus on building trust with partners and help their sellers leverage that trust. You might even call it spending trust. While Partner teams should be focused on creating and building trustworthy partner relationships and reciprocity, sellers should be the ones capitalizing on that trust.

## Care About What They Care About

When you get an introduction with the prospect, have a clear understanding of that contact's role and their individual needs. How is your solution going to improve their work as well as their company's success? By showing that you understand what they care about, you will be able to build a stronger relationship with them.

## Have a Strong Value Hypothesis

Understand why the account and contact you are attempting to engage with need you. You have a very short window of opportunity to get their full attention, so don't waste it on materials that don't apply to them. Make sure that you have a strong value hypothesis that speaks to their unique needs and challenges.

## Make It Easy for Them

Never, ever, ever ask for an intro where you have not already written an example intro for the person you are asking for an intro from. By making it easy for them to introduce you, you will be more likely to get their support. And once you have that support, you can start building a relationship with the prospect and working towards closing the deal.

With those tips in mind, let's get that intro.

Here's an "Intro" email template you can steal right now:

> "Hey [Contact Name], I've been in comms with [Prospect Contact(s)] over at [Prospect Account] the past [Few Weeks].
>
> I noticed [Your Relationship] with [Prospect Contact(s)], who I am trying to bridge the conversation over to.
>
> I am positioning [Value Proposition] as the reason for that conversation with them.
>
> Given your relationship, I'm reaching out with a draft email based on your feedback for an intro. I put a first draft with context on our previous comms below.
>
> Take a look and if you don't mind sending it over, will you let me know?
>
> In partnership,
>
> [Seller Name]
>
> [Email to be forwarded copy]
>
> P.S. It looks like we might share a handful of accounts/contacts I could intro you to as well I recently sold in [Relevant Industry Name]. Happy to discuss or help there if that's valuable, just lmk."

The beauty of this play and template is that it can be used for partners, customers, employee networks, advisors, investors, communities, and influencers—aka the total network of your company.

Of course, like the "influence" play, getting introductions requires some upfront work. Don't expect trust, whether in the form of intel, influence, or intros, to be given freely. When you are spending your partner's trust, show up having done the work that proves you are worthy of your ask.

Crafting a thoughtful intro email takes a bit of work, but so does building trust. This little bit of effort will get you more intros and more sales more of the time.

Not every intro attempt will succeed. There is a feedback loop on the nearbound account list with the AE, the sales manager, and the partner manager, to improve the process each time. For each successful attempt, analyze what worked. For each unsuccessful attempt, ask why you may have lacked the "trust funds" needed. Continuously refine your intro playbook *with your team*—not in isolation.

Intros are easily the most powerful play in all of sales, and the most effective use of my time day-to-day. Not all accounts or partners will be able to break you in, no matter how well you write an email, but practice makes perfect. I've honed this method so well over the years that 50% or more of the emails I write are emails for other people to send.

There's an art to knowing when you've built enough goodwill to make an ask. This art is akin to the "kinesthetic sense" that professional athletes develop, which instructs them on when to shoot, when to dribble, and when to pass. Remember that the partner intros play takes a team to run well. Prepare to be humbled if you're trying to win the game on solo three-pointers lobbed from half-court.

Once you customize and master this playbook, you'll start to see your network as your net worth, and you'll never think about selling the same ever again.

## Strategic Partners and the 3x5 Sales Strategy

Strategic partners require joint responsibility between sales and partnerships to drive sales impact. This section is not an essay on *"What is a strategic partner,"* but rather a qualifier to state what may not be obvious: *not all partners are strategic.*

The first reason I say this isn't for all partners is *time*. Aligning on a 3x5 strategy should be reserved for top current partners or top potential partners you, as a business, are fully committed to further activating. The second reason is *money*. You need to be talking material impact on some of your most important top prospective customers and accounts for all parties involved. This is an enterprise play at its core.

The 3x5 strategy was shared with me by Bobby Napiltonia who led the scaling of the global partner strategy for Salesforce directly under Marc Benioff. Bobby and his team minted, for instance, the Salesforce and Accenture partnership. He has three simple steps to run with five accounts across each step.

Use the 3x5 Strategy:

1. Identify your top 5 target accounts that are customers of your partner
2. Identify your partner's top 5 target accounts that are customers of yours
3. Identify your mutual top 5 new logos to pursue together

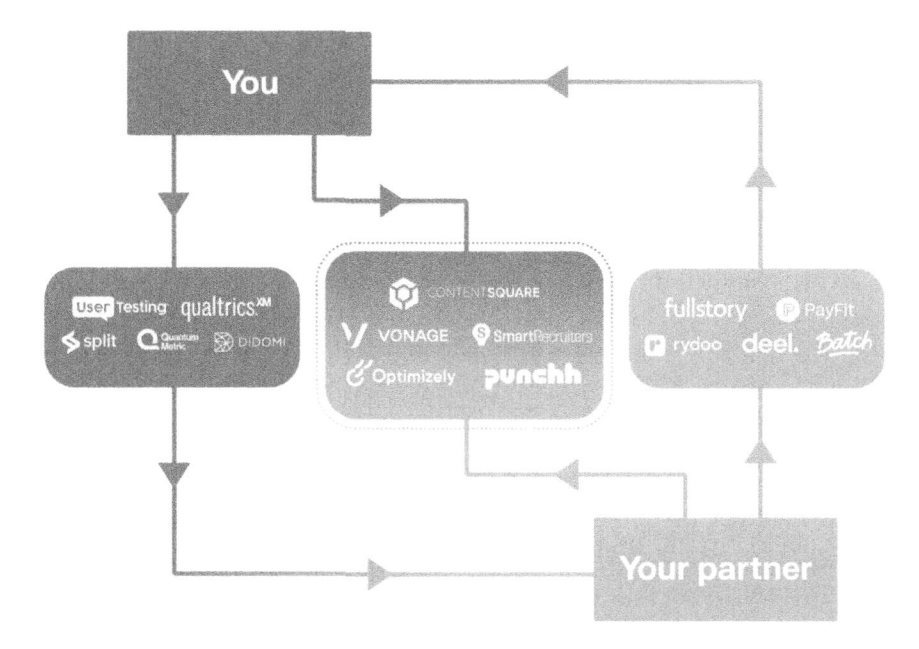

The 3x5 strategy is a way to both build and leverage trust for sales at the same time as your partners. In short, it's fair, and it's a great exercise to bring sales leadership at both teams into your most strategic shared accounts.

Sales leadership, partner managers, and partner marketers should collaborate on these accounts to:

- Develop succinct messaging and materials applicable to those accounts using nearbound intel.
- Create co-marketed campaigns that specifically target these accounts.
- Create honed-in value propositions, demos, and pitch scripts.
- Ensure that partners are getting wins on the accounts you've shared with them.

You will use intel, influence, and intros at each stage of the buyer's journey to win these specific accounts and help your partner do the same.

## Aligning Up the Chain

The 3x5 strategy can be an effective rep-to-rep strategy for strategic reps, but it's also important to proactively plan for executive alignment. Your strategy should include not just AE-to-AE collaboration, but also VP-to-VP.

Augmenting territory alignment is the best way to accomplish this. For example, after a few months of your AEs using a nearbound strategy on their accounts, you begin to see that two of them excel at working with a particular partner. They close every deal that this particular partner influences.

This is how executives can collaborate together to get more strategic. They can decide to put the AEs with high success levels on these joint accounts permanently and "re-segment" or "re-shuffle" territories to maximize impact.

This is something I did when I worked at Drift. I put 2 AEs I saw succeeding on all of the 6sense accounts, and they did the same. By doing so, 6sense's leadership and I were aligning on the long-term strategy of winning together and showing our commitment to this goal by redirecting our high-level resources.

## The Results

Think back to our beginning example of having 100 accounts and not knowing what the heck to do with them.

First, we asked: how do I prioritize these accounts?

Then we asked: what plays can I run to leverage the "3 I's of Nearbound" on these accounts?

With leadership in alignment, you're now asking: **where can we go from here?** You've seen the success, you're seeing the patterns, and now you're working together to leverage it for the long run.

So, what will the results look like if you follow this blueprint? Let's come back to our original goal of generating ⅓ of your total revenue from partnerships.

Let's say your organization has used inbound, outbound, and nearbound to collectively put 1,000 new prospects in your pipeline. Roughly 33% of those accounts have been prioritized using nearbound and the 3x5 strategy. Your team closes 200 accounts in total. But when you look at the data, you notice something incredible about the nearbound cohort:

- You saw a 2-3x higher win rate
- You closed them 35% faster than the other accounts
- You decreased your total CAC
- You increased your overall deal size
- Networking your CRM with partners, you were able to accurately track nearbound impact, making it easier for sales and partnerships teams to collaborate

In short, the nearbound accounts performed 2-3x better than the leads from inbound and outbound.

Where are these estimates coming from? This isn't rainbow-and-butterfly fiction. This is a very real and attainable outcome that hundreds of companies have already made happen by adopting a nearbound strategy. For example:

- Payfit had an increase of up to 60% in lead-to-demo conversion rate and an increase of up to 50% in demo-to-customer conversion rate.
- Rydoo had a 3x increase in pipeline.
- Contractbook generated 2x to 3x more demo meetings.
- AssessFirst had an increase of 4x in client integration and increased their lead generation by 100%.

Nearbound isn't just a strategy. It's a motion that's changing GTM forever. It's the augmentation of who you work with into your sales process, not just how you sell to them.

If you partner with those your buyers already trust for intel, influence, and intros you have a chance to lead the pack and outpace your competitors still stuck throwing more resources at outbound and inbound alone.

Rewind to my conversation with my friend, the Sales VP who had asked his team whether they could meet their sales target by achieving 100% of outbound sales targets (their answer was 'no').

He concluded our conversation on a more optimistic note, even though no one in leadership believes that in six months outbound or inbound performance will improve.

"The only effort correlated to impact right now is nearbound sales plays."

That's where we find ourselves.

Welcome to the Who Economy and the Nearbound Era.

May trust be your greatest asset and influence your greatest source of power. Seize the partner opportunity. Your company is counting on you.

But most importantly, so is the real boss: the customer. What will set you apart is a network of successful customers and partners who trust you.

# Part 4
## Nearbound Community

*"The most productive communities rally around a singular purpose. Partnerships professionals often get pigeonholed as 'relationships people' but that's not the case at all. We're revenue people who leverage relationships to move the needle. The key to making this work is to align both the individuals and the collective around the value we bring to each other and to the market. This is why I use a grassroots approach to execute nearbound. Because when you build trust with the individuals who make up your ecosystem by delivering consistently, you create an unstoppable community."*

— Rasheité (Radcliff) Calhoun,
Director of Channel Partnerships at Axios HQ

## CHAPTER 8

# SOCIAL SELLING 2.0

Working day to day with some of the brightest thinkers in B2B, like my mentors at Drift and PandaDoc taught me lessons that helped PartnerHacker (now nearbound.com) succeed from the start.

Among these luminaries, however, Jill stood out as a guiding star. Her LinkedIn profile was a true watering hole, bridging sales, martech, and the broader shift from brand marketing to digital marketing automation. But Jill was more than just a LinkedIn influencer. She was, as previously mentioned, the "Queen of Social Selling," a title earned through her mastery of give-first principles in communities like Eloqua. By profiling ideal customers, crafting tailored messaging, and surrounding them with value, Jill cultivated genuine reciprocity. Her ethos was simple yet profound:

"Show me you know me" and "Prove you care."

She redefined the salesperson's role into that of information concierge. Someone who guides buyers to exactly what they need. Jill's approach wasn't about competing for market share; it was about building trust and creating networks of mutual benefit.

November 2020 was a pivotal moment for me.

I knew the odds of success in launching a media company were slim. But I felt I had an unfair advantage that was still obscured to most—the power of partnerships and the leverage that comes from channeling the trust of those further along the trail. I invited Jill to share her insights on our fledgling podcast, PartnerUp (now the Nearbound Podcast). Despite her extensive interviews on sales, marketing, and social media, no one had yet prodded her to unveil the next chapter. No one was asking her the questions she really wanted to talk about—questions about what comes after the marketing automation revolution. Our 45-minute conversation gave Jill a stage to stitch together the patchwork of insights she had been dropping on social media.

Jill described surrounding customers with trusted advisors—blending sales, marketing, and success. She hinted at a new playbook founded on what she called "empathy technology." A marketplace of meaning to redeem the polluted data swamp.

That first podcast crystallized the pillars of the nearbound vision:

- The primacy of trust in human relationships
- Living in your market
- Selling *with* your closest partners

And the episode was a hit. By getting in front of Jill's network, she expanded the audience beyond my personal footprint. A single post by Jill received 10x to 20x more impressions, dwarfing our entire monthly traffic—all without any ad spend.

In the aftermath of the interview, I came to understand our aligned purpose, and my role became clear: to make those advancing our shared cause famous and act as if the world we imagined had already arrived.

My goal was to form a "conspiracy" in the best and truest sense of that word: a group of insiders who "breathe together" (*con spire*) to define the next era of business. To shift from isolation to integration. Monologue to dialogue. Noise to signal.

My reach was humble compared to Jill's. But I saw this as a feature, not a bug; with less reputation to risk, I could make bold bets and claims. I couldn't make her better known for the things she was already famous for, but I could amplify the signal of those things she now wanted to be known for: the things others weren't noticing or asking her about.

Rather than chase arbitrary metrics, I invested in trust.

## Nearbound Social: Timeless Principles for a Changing Landscape

For more traditional B2B companies and executives, social media strategy feels like a tightrope act—a delicate balance between safe (boring) and daring (risky).

The flip side of "going viral" is garnering fleeting fame for all the wrong reasons. As Warren Buffett said, "It takes 20 years to build a reputation, but only 5 minutes to ruin it."

You have to be especially careful of what my business partner Isaac calls ***algo simping***—contorting all your content in a desperate attempt to win the algorithm's favor and get more reach. The danger of algo simping is that the benefits are seen while the costs are unseen. It may drive up impressions or engagement, but it also works at diminishing your influence with the very types of decision-makers most valuable to your goals. When they see an obvious algo simp, they won't tell you or post a negative comment. They may even click the like button. But they also silently slot you into the "unserious attention-seeker" section of their mental filing cabinet.

And it's a never-ending game.

As soon as you step on the tightrope, the foundation beneath your feet starts shifting. LinkedIn tweaks its algorithm. What was cool last year is now cringe. Yesterday, it was Instagram carousels, YouTube Shorts, and Twitter threads. Today, it's "Threads" by Meta, Grok on X, and carousels on LinkedIn. The social media circus is chaotic enough to make anyone dizzy.

With the rise of AI and "DeSo" (decentralized social), it's impossible to predict what's coming next. TikTok AI filters that let you look and talk like your favorite influencers? Mixers hosted in the Metaverse?

In his 1912 seminal work, *Twelve Principles for Efficiency*, industrial engineer Harrington Emerson hinted at a better approach to social strategy and community building.

"As to methods there may be a million and then some," he wrote, "but principles are few. The man who grasps principles can successfully select his own methods. The man who tries methods, ignoring principles, is sure to have trouble."

Among these 12 principles are:

- **Clearly defined ideals:** Establishing a clear vision and purpose (Principle 1).
- **Discipline:** Methodical planning and execution of operations (Principle 4).
- **Standardization:** Uniformity in schedules, conditions, and procedures to ensure consistency (Principles 8-11).
- **Efficiency rewards:** Recognizing and rewarding contributions to productivity (Principle 12).

More than 100 years after Emerson wrote his management magnum opus, his principles are as relevant to B2B SaaS as to early 20th-century industrial engineering.

Nearbound social applies many of Emerson's timeless principles to orchestrate your entire organization's social activities to cut through the digital noise. You can stop with the "pray and spray" posting, hoping for viral hits, and start building a sustainable, principle-driven social media strategy.

The era of sales digitization and marketing automation gave us a powerful set of tools to interrupt consumers in their daily workflows with targeted Adwords, and more recently, promotions that show up right alongside pictures of their favorite influencer or nephew's graduation. It was inevitable that these tools would be used (and often abused) to their limits, leading to the great rift in trust we're living through today.

Instead of relying on intrusive and interruptive methods, nearbound social engages customers' attention and *intention*, without disrupting their daily lives. It does this by focusing more on *who* the message is coming from than how it's delivered.

As with nearbound sales and marketing, the nearbound social playbook is still evolving. Thankfully, we stand on the shoulders of giants like Jill, who have already outlined the core principles of the precursor to nearbound social found in social selling.

This section will equip you with tools and tactics to replicate what we started with PartnerHacker and continue now on a larger scale with nearbound.com. We are creating a community and a watering hole for the diverse trusted voices of the partnerships ecosystem—the same evangelists we identified in the marketing chapter.

Although we are a media company, we believe every company should be doing this through a mix of tactics: events, content creation, and targeted, coordinated social media campaigns.

## Social Selling 101

"Social selling" has become a buzzword. Google for tips on it, and you'll get pages of outdated sponsored content about how to optimize your profile, plus some boilerplate suggestions for engagement tools. More or less exactly what you would expect from the How Economy.

In the Who Economy, you need to be learning from those who have been to your promised land—not some freelance copywriter hired by a social listening platform trying to sell you their product. This crash course in social selling comes straight from the words of the Queen herself—distilled from her best writings, interviews, and social media posts.

Let's start with social selling in a sentence:

Social selling is about using social networks like LinkedIn and Twitter to forge genuine connections with buyers, influencers, and decision-makers.

Most sales and marketing teams view social media as advertising and promotion channels. But social selling, done right, is about nurturing relationships within your sales funnel through ongoing conversations.

Distinguishing between social media and social networks is pivotal. As Jill puts it, "Social media is about reach and marketing, while social networks are about cultivating relationships and sales." It's about being in the market, understanding buyers, and building trust. Living where your buyers are, and researching to understand their experience, what they care about, and who they listen to.

To be clear, social selling is *not* synonymous with social media marketing or advertising, which are increasingly zero-sum games. In the realm of social selling, we're not just capturing demand; we're generating it.

The efficacy of social networks isn't what it used to be. They are still vital tools, but they can't be the only ones. Why? Look no further than the cold outreach flooding LinkedIn DMs. These messages, often automated, masquerade as relationship-building but are just shortcuts.

Authentic social selling is grounded in the following five pillars:

- **Personal Credibility**: Establishing trust through authenticity and consistent value creation.
- **Always Be Connecting**: Building expansive networks and understanding the strength of connections.
- **Content is Currency**: Leveraging quality content to engage and build relationships.
- **Social Listening**: Tuning into the needs and voices of the audience for targeted engagement.
- **Measurement**: Assessing the effectiveness of social selling strategies through meaningful metrics.

Let's take them in turn:

## Personal Credibility

Social media has forced business interactions to become more human, even as fewer deals are happening in person. Celebrity influencers often engage with no-name accounts. Think of figures like Seth Godin or Arianna Huffington, who built their influence through direct, credible engagement. Their secret? They understood that people trust people, not faceless corporations. Seth hosts his blog at Seths.blog to put his personal identity front and center. Arianna Huffington named her company after herself and maintained her authentic authorial voice.

But paradoxically, while people are more connected, we also trust each other less than ever before. Trust is now the scarcest, most valuable commodity, and therefore, credibility is becoming more difficult to get.

Influencers conflate (and even try to game) popularity with credibility but going viral and being trusted are not the same thing.

Credibility cannot be gained overnight. The only way to get trust and credibility is through hundreds of interactions over time. Top social sellers aren't just pressing "post" on self-promotional content and then going about their day; they're consistently creating opportunities to have conversations that give to and engage the community. It's that opportunity to exchange meaningfully that brings credibility over time.

Credibility in this world comes from being authentically *you*. Auto DMs give off major robot vibes. A real profile picture isn't enough. Barbara Giamanco calls authentic social interaction "The New Handshake." With a well-executed social strategy, you can convey your humanity virtually at scale.

## Always Be Connecting

Glengarry Glen Ross taught us that ABC stood for "Always Be Closing." But today's customers don't want to be closed. They want to be helped when they're at the point of need and buy when they're ready to buy. You need to *Always Be Connecting*. Social selling is about fostering connections that go beyond mere transactions. In this era, the "strength of weak ties"—acquaintances and distant connections—plays a crucial role in gaining novel information and opportunities. Social selling thrives on the breadth and depth of your network.

Jill's mantra here is, "Know Thy Buyer." Understand their world, challenges, and goals. Position yourself as an educator, not a seller. Craft relevant messaging by researching buyers, influencers, and decision-makers, and aim to become "famous" among your niche—the smallest viable audience that gets your message. You don't need a Gary Vee-level follower count to nurture your niche. As Seth Godin says, everyone can become famous to 1,000 people.

Again, your network is your net worth.

And an organization's network value stems from its people.

As a leader, you need to encourage employees to share knowledge and messages within their networks. This helps increase connectivity within the organization and can give companies a competitive advantage. Social platforms allow employees to combine their unique knowledge into extraordinary collective intelligence. In remote and hybrid work settings, companies need to keep everyone connected through a shared mission and culture. It's not just about the work, but also about the relationships employees build with each other.

## Content is Currency

Content isn't just king—it's the currency of engagement. The quality, relevance, and consistency of your content dictate your success in building and sustaining relationships.

Everyone on your team can be a content creator. Social selling is a bridge between partnerships, sales, and marketing.

But not all content is created equal, especially when starting with a smaller audience. Major social media platforms only promote posts that meet specific criteria, usually those that keep users engaged on the platform. Try directing your LinkedIn followers to a self-promotional external link. That post is dead on arrival. Instead, nearbound utilizes social media to showcase your partners, your customers, and the people who already have trust in the market. You're creating content *with* and *from* them, processing them into their most shareable form, and then highlighting and tagging them on the platform itself.

## Social Listening

Amplifying others requires first listening deeply. You'll need a steady stream of evangelists to fuel your content engine. The question is: how do you identify these voices?

When Jill entered the VC world from sales, she started on Twitter—following a few seasoned investors and then following the influencers they engaged with. This created a "followship" that kept her feed filled with trending insights. She focused on understanding the connections between nodes and identifying strong ties within communities while bridging clusters through weak ties.

Instead of cold outreach with forced familiarity, learn to listen for signals of reciprocated interest. Note who engages with your content through likes or comments. This prevents wasted effort, as you learn which topics resonate *before* crafting content.

Remember: Most consumers are not on social media to look for stuff to buy. They go there for insight, entertainment, and information from people they trust.

Social selling in the Nearbound Era is about connecting consumers of social media with value via the people they trust. Tools like Hootsuite can be used to monitor Twitter and LinkedIn for specific mentions and pain points. Promptly respond with helpful solutions to build reciprocity.

## Measurement

Finally, even as we exit the era defined by Big Data, we must still heed the digits. Absent measurement, you operate blind. But not all data shed equal light on the success of your efforts.

Social sellers track two types of metrics: vanity and value. Vanity metrics include the Social Selling Index (SSI) calculated by LinkedIn, which quantifies your effectiveness on the platform across four dimensions. While higher scores correlate with sales success, they provide an incomplete picture and reveal little about actual deals influenced.

But if you're trying to justify the time you're spending on LinkedIn, you'll need to provide hard proof of ROI. This requires integration with other systems to connect social efforts to the bottom line.

Your CRM can be a valuable ally in measuring the success of your social selling efforts. By segmenting deals by source and adding "social selling" as an option, you can compare revenue from social leads with other channels. It's best to establish a baseline by tracking before launching a formal social selling program and then compare results quarter-over-quarter as your efforts grow. Keep in mind that initial numbers may not be impressive, as returns take time to manifest. However, there may be cases where a well-executed social play can lead to a significant surge in results, such as when our podcast downloads and email subscriptions skyrocketed after my first interview on partnerships with Jill.

Having watched Jill build a career atop these pillars, we were able to put them into practice from day one at nearbound.com, growing it into the number one partnerships media company. Jill and I have now both used this playbook to create new categories and shift the conversation in the B2B SaaS world away from the old inbound and outbound tactics to nearbound.

But our work isn't finished.

Nearbound social takes the principles of social selling beyond the sales department, making it a strategy woven throughout the entire company to gather relevant information about your buyers and buying committees, to engage with them, and to surround them with trust. Sales leadership has to drive the social selling initiative, but it won't gain traction without cooperation from marketing.

## The Nearbound Social Playbook

The rules of nearbound social are changing all the time. But you can still practice the fundamentals.

This section will equip you with tools and tactics to replicate at scale what's worked for us at nearbound.com and for me personally throughout my career.

We aren't making random, sporadic attempts to insert ourselves into trending topics; we are producing enough quality social content to set trends, not just follow them.

The most successful social media personalities did not achieve fame through blind luck or raw talent. They followed timeless principles—the same ones Harrison Emerson outlined back in 1908, namely, defining your ideals and mission, and discipline—or making plans and running operations accordingly.

This section covers tactical advice to illustrate the core concepts of nearbound social. The tactics themselves may change over time as platforms and algorithms shift, but the overarching ethos will continue enabling relationship-driven growth.

Remember, this playbook cannot be an isolated effort. Social media is one of the few areas where your entire organization can work across departmental lines.

## The Power of Partner Social Proof

Whenever we think we have come up with a novel idea, it's good consult with Robert Cialdini, the preeminent prophet of persuasion. Usually we are reminded that there really is nothing new under the sun.

Take social proof. Cialdini codified the core tenets of social proof decades ago, yet brands still "discover" this lever as if uncovering lost scrolls of an ancient sage. Social proof is the phenomenon in which people look to others for guidance and follow the herd when they lack sufficient information to judge a situation. It holds a powerful sway over human behavior, especially amidst uncertainty. If people witness their peers pursuing a course, they follow the herd. In his seminal work *Influence*, Cialdini relays a story of New Yorkers asked to conserve energy during a shortage. Those informed of how much energy their neighbors conserved reduced usage more than those simply asked to save power. People follow the crowd. If others act, we assume their choice is wise.

Marketers leverage this herd instinct by showcasing what "others like you" are doing. Testimonials, reviews, and case studies are all forms of social proof saying, "You can trust us, too."

Yet brands often underestimate social proof's gravitational pull. They fail to harness partners beyond asking for clumsy product plugs. Partners should be thought of as relays amplifying your signal across their trusted networks. This requires a regular rhythm of value-driven content. Keep the focus on their message and your aligned narrative. Once you establish credibility, then you can promote keystone content to catalyze real-world action.

For example, when promoting an event on LinkedIn, ask a participating partner to comment on the post with the registration link, saying that they just registered and encouraging others to follow suit. This quickly imbues your post with third-party validation.

Wielding social proof skillfully also builds partner trust. If you demonstrate that you will make them look good first, they will be more likely to share content and grant you access to their following. Thus social proof fuels a flywheel effect. You spotlight partners, expanding their reach and brand. Reciprocally, their promotion attracts new followers to your ecosystem.

## A Nearbound Community Content Pyramid

At nearbound.com, our strategy centers around three different kinds of activities for tying together the content and the community to create social network effects:

1. Pillar Content
2. Window Content
3. Events

We'll start unpacking pillar content because it's the year-round constant element that anchors our strategy, driving engagement and building relationships within and beyond our community.

## Pillar Content

We start by collaborating on in-depth pillar content like podcasts, long-form articles, or analyses of studies and publishing of reports, from which other content will be derived. Pillar content is designed to both draw and maintain attention. Our mission and values provide a foundation, and our social media provides the decoration or "window dressings," but the pillar content holds up the entire structure. If you can't produce pillar content that drives conversations within your community or others, your house won't stand for long.

Video podcasts are one of our favorite formats for pillar content. It is much easier to ask a partner to participate in a quick conversation in a virtual studio to capture their recent insights, rather than requesting them to write a guest blog post or article. By presenting the content in both podcast and article formats, we make it valuable for both those who prefer to listen for an hour or read for 10 minutes.

The team at nearbound.com uses Riverside.fm to record interviews for both audio and video in high-definition, which we post along with the transcripts and takeaways as part of our core pillar content. Our goal with pillar content is twofold: we strive to make conversations more relevant and the cadence predictable to build our nearbound house, and we want to find the signals that allow us to create more pillar content.

## Window Content

While pillar content is what holds everything together, you can't make all of your content pillar content. Most of it has to be "window content," or micro-content, to make it possible for people to want to peer inside. Pillar content should be broken down into its best social snippets. The flashy "ahas!" and moments worth sharing need to be carved out and developed as a continuation to maximize reach and attention. Great pillar content should be turned into great window content.

When you have a solid piece of pillar content, you can repurpose the best moments into many pieces of micro-content—shorter snippets of the long-form article or podcast that you turn into memes, quotes, newsletter blurbs, or stories. If you have a podcast, for example, you can generate multiple shorter clips from the same episode. Post the clip with a teaser, summary, or particularly quotable line, and tag the partner or evangelist you're featuring. Look for the moments that will resonate most with your audience—moments of particular emotional or insightful resonance.

We create a good chunk of our micro-content using Descript, a user-friendly video podcast editor, as well as Canva. These apps and their AI allow us to extract snappy clips with captions and design graphics and carousels featuring the most resonant quotes or insights based on the actual voices of the community.

The key is letting partners share their unfiltered perspectives through pillar content, then strategically repurposing it to reinforce your narrative in a way that *makes them look like the hero*. Don't force plugs of your product. Think instead as if you're creating the highlight reel of the stories or advice on navigating the path to the promised land. Think like a media company if you want to drive conversations on social media.

Gary Vee calls this the "content pyramid" (hence the name for this section). Pillar content, like his daily vlog, feeds micro-content across all of his social media channels, which ultimately drives viewership back to the foundational long-form video content on YouTube.

You can then distribute the micro-content across social platforms, tagging partners and evangelists to engage their networks. Think of your evangelists as nodes of trust; they are not "just a channel." Your partners should be eager to share concise, professional videos of themselves, edited down to remove any unnecessary content. They can also write a LinkedIn post in their own voice, which will further build trust with their audience.

The added bonus is that if you consistently post helpful content, the algorithm notices and begins amplifying its organic reach. Even better, you can multiply that effect through other voices as well. Social networks in B2B are also paying attention to this phenomenon. As of writing, LinkedIn is testing the ability of some brands to boost high-potential posts with their own thought leader ads.

The tools will evolve, but the principles endure. Work with your partners to create pillar content and make it look great by sharing valuable content. Show them you care while co-creating and sharing ideas aligned with your strategic vision and narrative of the promised land. Help first, and the returns will follow.

But when it comes to nurturing social connections and building a community, the true foundation of the pyramid is events. Let's think bigger to create experiences that enable even more impactful pillar content and micro-content.

## Events: The Foundation for Your Content Pyramid

As you invest in and expand your nearbound marketing and community, few initiatives can be more appropriate or impactful than events. If you want to ignite perpetual growth in the Nearbound Era, don't ignore events and never do them alone. As Tyler Calder, the CMO of PartnerStack, told me after executing a 1,500-person event with us, "I'll never do another event alone."

Let's unpack.

First, events create a forcing function that drives commitment from both your company and partners to show up and deliver value *on a specific day*. There's a public deadline. The stakes are raised when reputations are on the line. To host or attend an event, you have to care. If you want others to show up, you have to make them care in advance, by structuring the event around shared values (read: not your product launch or latest feature or case study).

Second, events provide measurable outcomes tied to your goals—in terms of reach, attendees, subsequent sign-ups, sales leads, demos, or big deals influenced. You should structure the event to gain clarity on what moves the needle, rather than just hoping your message resonates.

Events also offer real-time feedback on which experiences and content are resonating with your audience. You can observe reactions in the room, chat comments, and debates that spring out to hone your narrative. From this feedback, you can further discussions and create keynotes that generate the most buzz or impressions on social media surrounding the event.

Within a marketing context, the most important point to remember when hosting an event is that your role is to facilitate—to empower partners to contribute *their* expertise and stories to lay a path to your customers' promised land. You are producing an experience that transforms your partners' influence into outcomes. Like any facilitator, make the speakers shine rather than yourself. When producing a nearbound event, remember this: *the event **is** the product.*

Events also build community and reinforce shared beliefs. Attendees realize that they are part of something bigger than themselves. There is no faster way to build a movement and ignite exponential growth. Events bring together your ecosystem into a watering hole to network and build bonds face-to-face. As Mark Kilens notes, "Humans have always been about getting together into tribes. No one wants to go off and be alone, and the right events fulfill our innate human need for connection."

If you need proof that events should be your number one partnership play, look no further than the energy in the room when you bring together the right people around the right stories. Events satisfy the fundamental human desire to connect with others who share our values and are working towards a better future. What could be a more powerful catalyst for understanding your growth? Events that meet the promise of nearbound marketing leave everyone with a feeling they can't shake—and an excitement that carries momentum.

## Supercharge Your Narrative

If you want to maximize impact, events can't just be generic tactics in your marketing toolkit. If you think of an event just in terms of generating sales leads, it will be obvious to your audience that they are being set up for a hard pitch. Likewise, your partners will see through your intentions and won't commit themselves or care to lend their voice to your strategic narrative.

The most successful events activate your ecosystem by connecting participants on a values level.

As Mark Kilens told me during the 2022 Nearbound Summit, "The best partnerships are rooted in a shared belief system and vision of the future."

It was that shared vision that brought Mark and 120+ speakers and panelists together for a week-long virtual event attended by 5k+ people from every corner of GTM and the world. That's where we declared that partnerships shouldn't just be a department, but a strategy for every department. And we brought together the voices from every department. It sparked our movement around a unified vision and voice.

So, before planning any event, clarify your strategic narrative and objectives. Then structure an experience tailored to the specific audience segments and partners who will help manifest that vision.

This also aligns with the nearbound marketing methodology we outlined in Phases 1 and 2. You must intimately understand your Ideal Customer Profile, crafting a story that resonates with their worldview. Events offer a compelling format to leverage what you've learned about that worldview and express your narrative to a captive, engaged audience.

Effective narratives also tie back to your overall company growth strategy and objectives. What specifically are you trying to achieve in the next quarter and year?

For example, your strategy may be penetrating a new niche customer segment this year. In that case, an event tailored specifically to that audience and their pain points will prove far more effective than a generic conference presence trying to attract a wide swath.

An event rooted in shared values can and should still be structured with tangible goals for your company. As Bryan Brown, Co-Founder & Chief Analyst at GTM Partners, advises, "You need to know what you're trying to accomplish with the event."

As another example, a small local user group event allows more high-touch conversations to identify promising leads. This can feed into a larger regional event focused on booking meetings and demonstrating your solution. Finally, an annual conference with key partners closes deals through tailored breakout sessions and high-touch more intimate experiences as offshoots of the stages.

No matter the format, avoid being generic, and don't forget the main reasons why you and everyone else are there. Attendees are trying to reach the promised land and want to be around those who've already been there. Many events fail by trying to be everything to everyone—ending up irrelevant to anyone. Intentionally design each element to propel attendees towards an outcome.

This applies to partners as well. Provide clear expectations on roles and goals upfront. Make it clear that you want their expertise—not their sponsorship or endorsement of your product. With an aligned purpose, they can activate their network pointed towards shared objectives.

The energy in the room will feel palpable.

## Supercharge Your Brand

Jill stresses that "every interaction leaves a brand impression." This maxim rings especially true for events, where the event brand comes to life across dozens of touchpoints. Your event brand should not be your corporate brand. This is not "AcmeCo Annual" speaking here, it's the watering hole for your community. Before you ever get to "activation," all great change requires "inspiration."

That is where your event brand comes in. Obvious examples can be found with Salesforce's "DreamForce," or Microsoft's "Inspire," but also in every aspect of the event experience. From the registration process to signage, to the virtual vibe, to swag bags, treat each element as an opportunity to embody your values and strategic narrative. Attendees notice when you cut corners to serve your product and not *them*.

Consistency across touchpoints reinforces your credibility and memorable brand association—experiences are *felt* and *lived*.

Use your strategic narrative as a litmus test. Does the messaging on event promotion align with positioning on signage and programs? Do partner contributions illustrate your values and echo the promised land of the community you're gathering? Are you making others famous, or just shining the spotlight on yourself?

With careful orchestration, you transform an event from a standalone tactic into an immersive brand experience. Attendees become embedded in your vision of the future. The energy and community outlive the event. Attendees realize they've been a part of something special.

They eagerly become brand evangelists, organically amplifying your strategic narrative across their networks. This is how you strengthen your brand's gravitational pull—getting physically closer to your partners and attracting their audience into your own orbit.

That is the difference between a product event centered around *you* and a nearbound event centered around *them*.

## Supercharge Attention and Intention

Mark Kilens talks about the opportunity events offer to blend both attention and *intention*. And I trust him here—he was the mastermind behind HubSpot's Academy, Drift INSIDER, CMO of Airmeet, and now CEO of Tack. He's been to the promised land of events, community, and partnerships (and I've been fortunate enough to be a part of these experiences with Mark on several occasions). In short, Kilen's point is that attracting an audience through promotion and content creates *attention*. But the event experience then converts interest into action or *intention*.

For example, a keynote may spark initial curiosity about an idea. But the magic happens, too, in the hallway, where attendees are debating implications and what new steps they might take on their path to their promised land, as well as who they're following, imitating, or paying to help them make those moves.

Poll questions are one powerful way to guide this journey from attention to intention. Polls work especially well in multi-person panels, where each partner can contribute a tailored poll question to get a pulse of the audience. This provides each of your partners the opportunity to conduct their real-time market research and gives a wider spectrum of feedback for you to analyze afterward.

When polling the audience, avoid overly marketing-focused questions. Don't try to gauge their interest level in your product. People don't like feeling marketed to. They want to feel heard and understood.

Instead, use these poll questions as conversation starters. Ask for opinions, perspectives, and challenges faced. Their answers will then provide the context to determine how to make follow-up conversations that could yield an actual conversion. In today's marketing, the metric isn't the method. The customer is at the center, and a conversation is the best outcome you can work toward—with the attention and intention of a potential customer.

Poll responses can also reveal gaps between perceptions and reality. For example, an audience poll may indicate the audience tends to favor integration ease of use when buying a product but underestimates the benefit of their integration strategy. Of course, I'm using this example because it's one I've used. When we shared the results back during the event, the sentiment was clear: the way we're buying has changed, but the way we're building hasn't caught up—the very inspiration for change. Attendees felt more connected to making change because they didn't feel alone. They felt understood, and in turn, the conversations we and our partners had after the event ended up converting much more than otherwise.

You earn *intention* by respecting *attention*.

And of course, never forget the fun parts. Consistently look for ways to make events an exchange of ideas that create moments of surprise, intrigue, insight, or delight. Have partners co-develop content and sessions based on audience input before the event. Release entirely new content products to the audience—real pillar content. Make the event "where" people want to make moments happen with and beside you. You can even make the audience a part of the experience, too. Create moments that make people say, "You *had to be there,*" or "You *gotta see this.*"

## Concluding with the GOAT of Pyramid Content

No one gets this more than Harry Mack.

Harry Mack, that freestyle guy?

Yes. Harry was one of 2023's biggest sensations on tour, YouTube, and TikTok. And, in my humble opinion, the greatest freestyle artist of all time. But his genius isn't just in the mastery of his art—you might be able to argue that 'X' or 'Y' freestyle artist could top Harry Mack in some ways, but it's undeniable where he's the most genius. Foundation and event content (tours), pillar content (YouTube Channel), and window or micro content (TikTok or YouTube Shorts).

Harry's genius is that for every single thing he touches when he freestyles, he involves the audience right then and there in that moment. Whether it's on his hit series *Omegle Bars* where he releases entire rap songs using a few random words each from strangers on the internet, to his truly one-of-a-kind concerts where he freestyles entire performances based on concepts and words texted by the audience to a screen behind him, to the mega-viral TikToks with millions of views, Harry isn't just the GOAT of freestyle: he's the goat of pyramid content.

Watching Harry do this is more like watching your favorite athlete than it is watching a concert. Just like every game is a new experience, so is following Harry. It's not the same stuff on repeat. It's the live game, the post-game coverage, and the clips.

Harry is *partnering* with the audience in real-time.

I got to see the impacts firsthand as we brought Harry into the Nearbound Summit in 2023, and he created a truly unforgettable collaborative experience.

If you want to create content that creates community, build a strong foundation that brings people together, construct pillars that keep the house strong, and clip window content for the highlight reels.

# Part 5

# Nearbound Customer Success

*"The best companies have identified the close correlation between adoption of their partner integrations and increased customer retention. They also know a customer is much more likely to successfully implement and adopt their product if there is an expert consulting partner guiding them through the process.*

*One of the smartest things a customer success organization can do to increase customer engagement and retention is to systematically identify where they have overlapping customers with partners and encourage adoption of integrations and additional partner services. We continue to hear huge wins from members of the Partnership Leaders network who have used this strategy."*

—Asher Mathew, Co-founder & CEO of Partnership Leaders

CHAPTER 9

# TYING SUCCESS WITH THE SERVICING BOWTIE

Remember the old days when software came in a box? Those rainbow iridescent discs represent a simpler time when you could hold a product in your hands. Those of us who are old enough remember the feeling of tearing through the plastic wrapping to load the installation disc, watching the progress inch along, then, after a long wait, success! The program would be ready to use on your very own personal computer.

Sure, it was clunky compared to slick modern SaaS apps, but consumers figured it out and loved the process. For businesses making investments in tech, it wasn't as simple as loading and installing a program. It wasn't just one computer, it was many computers, local networks, servers, and even large-scale physical hardware (e.g., telephony infrastructure). These physical constraints often resulted in a "channel" of local distributors, vendors, and partners who marketed, sold, and serviced the purchase—all in one.

Back then, businesses invested big bucks upfront when purchasing software alongside hardware—usually in the form of a perpetual license. Software vendors sent experts to set everything up, provide detailed training, and hold the customers' hands through the installation, configuration, upkeep, and maintenance. Customer service meant patient, personal support until you were off and running.

Today, businesses get instant access to the latest tools and updates in the cloud with a few clicks. If it's not meshing with their workflows, they can switch providers with just a few more clicks. As a result, software companies can no longer rest easy after securing the initial purchase. Now, the relationship resets every year, quarter, or month when your subscription is up for renewal. Customers expect rapid onboarding and continuous improvement balanced with stability and round-the-clock support from service teams who know our unique needs.

Customer success is no longer a static achievement reached once the software is installed and functioning. The shift towards Software as a Service (SaaS) is the reason *customer success* became a department. As the name suggests, modern software is more of a service than a product. Success may look like a noun, but SaaS companies have shifted to a dynamic approach defined by verbs like integrating, educating, training, supporting, and retaining. In this world, success is an action—a continuous provision of value. In a word, *servicing*. For Customer Success Managers (CSMs), servicing means identifying ways to improve each customer's experience as their needs evolve. When account mapping software reveals new intelligence—for example, that five customers just purchased software from an integration partner—CSMs must be able to connect the dots in real-time and be proactive, not just reactive to customer support inquiries.

Customer success requires more than just understanding your own company's software. That's table stakes. In the Nearbound Era, customer success is about understanding your customers and the world they inhabit. The stakes have been raised. Your customer's problems are your problems. That's not to say the perpetual license model in years past meant companies or their channel partners *didn't* understand their customers. It's only to say that, more than ever, your product is not what matters. What matters is the success of your customers—every day, month, quarter, and year.

It doesn't matter how many partners you have if you can't solve your customers' problems and help them get to the place they're trying to go.

No matter how good your product marketing is, your customer's success no longer depends solely on your product. Your success, and theirs, is tied to a plethora of other technology companies and the partners they utilize.

According to a 2023 Productiv press release, the average enterprise in 2023 used more than 473 SaaS applications, a staggering increase of 156 from the 317 they were using in 2021.

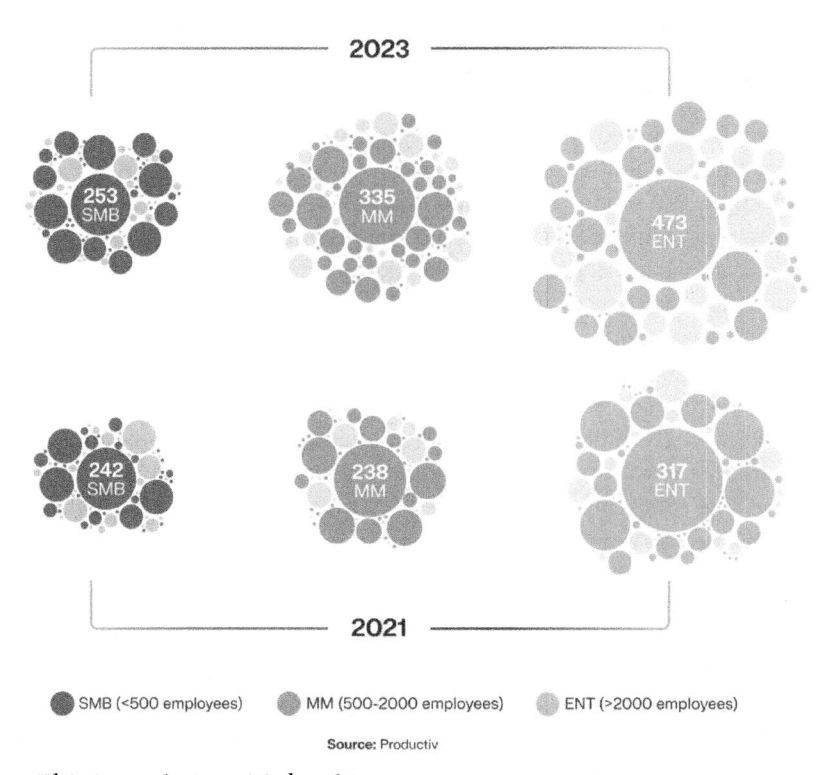

[Figure: Bubble chart comparing number of SaaS apps by company size in 2023 (253 SMB, 335 MM, 473 ENT) versus 2021 (242 SMB, 238 MM, 317 ENT). Legend: SMB (<500 employees), MM (500-2000 employees), ENT (>2000 employees). Source: Productiv]

This is so obvious it's hard to see.

You are **one** of those 473. *One.*

In the Nearbound Era, customer success is officially and inextricably tied to "who": who they use, who they trust, who helps them, and who else is touching on the same challenges your customer faces. It's about understanding and solving your customers' 7,478 problems *with* the technologies and service providers they trust.

Despite the complexity of the problem, the solution turns out to be easier than it looks. Let's break it down.

## Learning to Get Out of the Way to Make Room for Partners

Imagine you run a company that sells MarTech software. Your end customer is a VP of Marketing or Chief Marketing Officer.

You might have a kick-ass CSM who has been with the company for several years and they know your company's product inside out.

Still, they are maybe three to five years out of college, and you're putting them in a room with an executive. Has your CSM ever been a CMO? They've never walked a mile in the customer's shoes. They have never been to the customer's promised land. Given the complex constellation of intertwined products and business challenges, CSMs cannot know everything about the customer or their 473 products, use cases, and objectives. As the queue of customer questions and service demands grows, it becomes clear that it is not feasible to provide the specialized solutions that today's customers expect with entry-level talent.

But how will you attract top talent and consultants to work in your professional services org, when they're already making far more money working for the big systems integrators, agencies, or other tech consulting firms?

You won't. But you can still bring them into the mix. They are your partners. Your customer's partners. Those who surround the customer not only with the technology but also with the services to drive their desired *outcomes* from the software. The trick is to provide customers with the right service partners to activate what Winning By Design refers to as "The Recurring Revenue Bowtie."

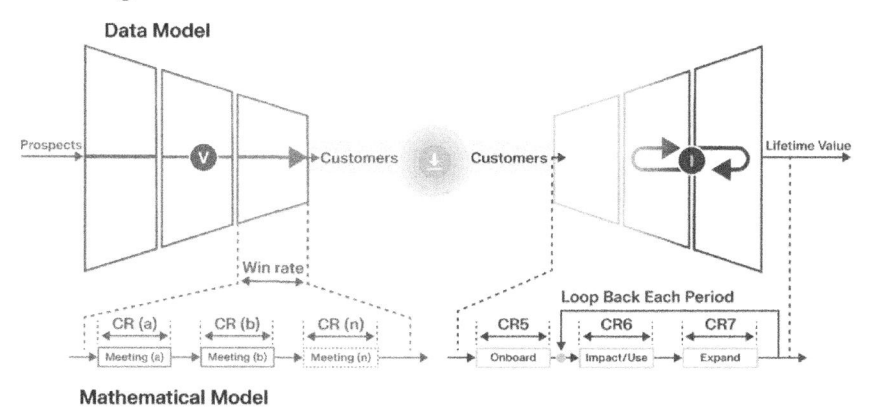

*The Recurring Revenue Bowtie.* **Credit**: *"The Operating Model for Recurring Revenue." Winning by Design. June 2022.*

The Bowtie is distinguished by two major motions: the first half focuses on volume (V)—driving growth by making small improvements at each of the key moments in the customer acquisition process. The second half of the Bowtie focuses on impact (I), or driving compound growth by making small improvements at each of the key moments in the customer success process (such as onboarding, renewal, cross-sell, and upsell). Looking at their model through a nearbound lens, we can see that each conversion step (labeled in the diagram as "CR") can include partner influence to drive success. But if you're only focusing on bringing partners in to grow, but not to keep, your company isn't going to last long.

Unlike SaaS companies or ISVs, a service firm does not sell access to technology but instead focuses on delivering outcomes: solution-oriented services based on intellectual property that help customers win. When customers hire agencies to help them reach their goals, the agencies are often more invested in achieving those goals than the customers themselves — and certainly more invested in doing so than the ISV. Customers don't care about your sales volume; they care about their own impact.

While you may tout the potential impact or solutions your software provides, it's rare for a service contract to directly link your Annual Recurring Revenue (ARR) to the tangible outcomes experienced by the customer. In contrast, service firms and partners typically engage in contracts that are outcome-based, ensuring their vested interest aligns with achieving—or surpassing—the goals set by the customer.

Often the greatest obstacles to effectively servicing customers stem from a defensive company culture that clings to the old model, guarding their share of revenue and perceived "ownership" of customer accounts.

To put it plainly: In the Nearbound Era, you do not own the customer or their dollars. Instead, think of yourself as renting space in the customer's world. In this arrangement, you're not the landlord, the customer is. Your software or services are essentially the rent you pay for occupying a position in their market space. If the enterprise value of their space is not increasing, you shouldn't be surprised that yours isn't either.

Vendors and agencies already have trusted relationships with your customers. They, too, are renters in the customer's space, contributing their own unique value. The customer retains ultimate ownership of their accounts, not you. You must let go of the illusion that you're in charge of "your" accounts. They are in charge of themselves. You are a piece of the puzzle—if you are lucky.

Ignoring the other parties who also rent from the customer is a surefire path toward eviction. Don't be afraid of the other tenants. Instead, embrace them and understand how they contribute to a whole which is greater than the sum of its parts.

If your business feels threatened by your partners' knowledge, earned experience, technical understanding, empathy for the customer, or their ability to understand the big picture, then it may be time to reconsider the name of the department responsible for "customer success." If you can't put wins on the board with the vendors and service providers (aka partners) who already have a relationship with your customers, then you have no business being a customer success professional.

Competing with partners who have the solutions your customer needs has no place in the nearbound universe. Ford and GM could have refused the olive branch from Tesla to join its supercharger network, strengthening the value of the EV ecosystem as a whole. Instead, their CEOs chose cooperation where everyone benefited from the network effects. Owners of Ford and GM vehicles will enjoy premium service for the products they purchased without those companies having to lift a finger.

Of course, many CS veterans have been burned by poorly executed partnerships. To some, nearbound customer success may sound like a euphemism for "outsourcing." Outside consultants and agencies—when improperly aligned to customer outcomes that can be at odds to the ISV's desires—can create more headaches and support tickets for your team. The beauty of nearbound is that it transforms existing hazards into opportunities. By providing a proper knowledge base, training programs, and overlay model, your partners can work hand-in-glove with customer service departments. This frees your team to focus on orchestrating the overall customer journey that drives your company revenue without the impossible burden of understanding the hundreds of software vendors, service partners, and interconnections within the customer's environment. The CS department becomes the crucial staging ground and incubator for some of your company's most important partnerships.

## The Power of Agency Partners

Justin Gray is an entrepreneur with a track record of building partner-led businesses over the past two decades. He served as the CEO of LeadMD (prior to its acquisition by Shift Paradigm) and later founded In Revenue Capital. His mission at LeadMD was to assist companies in leveraging the growth of marketing automation platforms such as Marketo.

The limiting factor in utilizing these platforms was not the product itself. Marketo helped bring marketing automation to almost any company that invested in learning the product, implementing best practices, and staffing roles such as marketing ops, demand generation, and content marketing. The bottleneck existed in the talent required to leverage the platforms. In the early 2010s, these were all new functions. Justin and his team provided the necessary expertise through their agency's services. In fact, they did so for over 3,000 Marketo customers during their decade-plus working relationship.

For Marketo, Justin and his team were a perfect solutions partner. His company shared an ideal customer profile, possessed complementary strengths, and provided a compelling joint solution. Most importantly, however, Justin had a strong belief in the power of partnerships.

Although LeadMD specialized in helping customers orchestrate an automated customer journey, most of their leads came from a different source. They received more than double the bookings from nearbound deals sourced through their partners like Marketo than through their own marketing automation. In the early days, Justin learned to treat these super-partnerships like a startup unto itself—getting alignment across the organizations on goals and strategy alongside their ISV partners to drive customer outcomes.

LeadMD created a new business unit internally called "packaged services." Every time Marketo sold a deal, Marketo also sold a service package on Marketo paper. Who delivered that service package? LeadMD—thousands of times.

Marketo still assigned CSMs to every account that LeadMD serviced. LeadMD wasn't responsible for outsourced customer success, they overlaid and worked *with* the customer success manager. And it worked for *everyone*. LeadMD succeeded, Marketo succeeded, Marketo's CSMs succeeded, but most importantly, the customer succeeded.

While it may seem counterintuitive, relinquishing some control through collaboration empowers your customer success team to gain more control over the outcomes that matter: retention and expansion of happy customers. Partners enable you to concentrate resources on the highest priorities and generate leverage where your CSMs lack experience and expertise.

But you must be selective, choosing partners who deliver the most valuable ongoing servicing. Success is not just short-term wins—it's about making a small number of strategic decisions to spin a flywheel into motion.

## CHAPTER 10

# FROM BOWTIE TO FLYWHEEL

When it comes to SaaS, Brian Balfour, CEO of Reforge and former VP of Growth at HubSpot said it best: "If your retention is poor, nothing else matters."

While Account Executives or Account Managers may handle upsells, the customer success team ensures that existing customers are maximizing the value of your software and services. This, in turn, tees up the renewal and is the primary influence on whether they upgrade their subscription.

Yet customer success is viewed as a net drain. Most large SaaS companies have internal professional services organizations that are set up to offset the costs of servicing customers—at a cost to the end customer. While these extensions of customer success generate revenue, they are generally not a profit center. Even when they break even, they can hurt the P&L and reflect poorly on the unit economics of the business.

**Here's why:** Many boards, CFOs, and public market investors often rely on simple indicators within the P&L. One of the most commonly used indicators is the Cost of Goods Sold (COGS). COGS encompasses the total cost of developing and maintaining the software for the customer. This includes not only direct expenses such as hosting and software fees paid by the vendor, but also the salaries of customer support and professional services staff.

For most best-in-class SaaS companies, COGS is around 10-20% of revenue. Operating at break-even appears as a loss because it brings down the company's gross margin of 80-90%. This hurts the financial performance of the business since customer support is a fixed cost on your books.

However, when budgets are tight and it is harder to land new deals, it is even more imperative to deepen relationships with existing customers. By the time your product comes up for renewal, the outcome should be a foregone conclusion—not a moment of anxiety for your sales team. Proving your value and upselling to your existing customers represents the most capital-efficient form of ARR with the best unit economics.

Asher Matthew, the CEO & Co-Founder of the world's largest partnerships community, Partnership Leaders, doesn't mince words about understanding the unit economics of your business.

"CFOs do not care about any type of partner influence," he says.

"The way they speak is through a Profit & Loss (P&L) statement, and on a P&L statement, there's no category for partner influence."

Thus, the focus of a nearbound CSM should not be expanding the employee count of their department and providing the most services internally. It should be nurturing relationships and surrounding customers with expertise—especially when that means going outside the boundaries of their organization.

What if your professional services are fulfilled by partners?

No fixed cost. Higher gross margins. Better cost structure and capital efficiency. And the list goes on. That's the language of the CFO. Learn to speak the language of the P&L, and your company, your partners, and your career will thank you.

According to Canalys, companies with strong partner programs enjoy a 15% higher renewal rate and a 20% increase in upsell revenue. Forrester Consulting finds that partnered vendors have 10% higher customer lifetime value and nearly 14% lower churn. Even more dramatically, Forrester also finds that customers who work with partners are 57% more likely to renew their contracts.

When churn is high, it's tempting to hoard service revenue internally by throwing more bodies at the problem. But expanding your in-house service team distracts from the bigger picture: the surrounding ecosystem, and the flywheel that brings more partners and customers. Not only do your unit economics like gross margin improve, but you turn the bowtie turned flywheel.

Your sales team wins because renewals are automated. The product team wins because customer feedback reveals new feature ideas and integration opportunities. Sales and marketing win when they can transform a successful customer story into a case study, elevating both the partner and the customer. And lastly, partners win through expanded business driven by your recommendations.

All of these wins start with shaping your customer success department into a lean, mean servicing team with compound interest.

Funnel-based businesses are faucets: stop filling them and you lose. Bowtie businesses are better businesses where dollars go farther. But flywheels are the perpetual motion machine of SaaS.

Just ask Microsoft. At their 2023 annual event, CEO Satya Nadella talked about Microsoft's creation of **$6,500,000,000,000.00** in ecosystem value. That's not a typo. Yes, $6.5 trillion. With a T.

Under Nadella's leadership, Microsoft embraced 100% partner attach. They led the way in transforming GTM strategies and product development. The results? A complete company turnaround and, of course, now, the largest B2B company in the world, and only second to Apple with consumers (as they battle it out above $3T in market cap on any given day at the time of writing).

And the most impressive part? Achieving this at an accelerated speed, despite its unbelievable size. At that annual event, he called for an additional $2.5 trillion of ecosystem value created solely from their AI strategy with partners. His journey is proof of partnership success on an unimaginable scale, compounded by network effects that yield increasing dividends over time. He thinks in terms of flywheels, not funnels, and operates in perpetual motion, not fluid dynamics.

$5 trillion of the 6.5 trillion in value will be created by their partners working on top of their solution. In other words, it's ecosystem value, not Microsoft value. Your product alone—without an ecosystem of partners surrounding it—is worthless. You grow the pie by connecting customers to communities, agencies, integrators, and support specialists within your ecosystem.

Nadella's nearbound flywheel story proves the old saying: "If you want to go fast, go alone. If you want to go far, go together."

His unwavering dedication to Microsoft's partner ecosystem is a masterclass in leadership, redefining how we perceive growth and success. His story is our story (and it just happens to be the biggest story). If the most important CEO at the most rapidly innovating (and largest) company in the world can't convince you that the Nearbound Era has arrived, nothing will.

## Leading Customer Success with Partnerships: Building a Certification Program at Drift & The Pirate Island Problem

While serving as the Global Head of Partnerships at Drift, I became convinced that to make a partner successful on the agency, solution, or service side, we had to embed the partner solutions program within the customer success department. In fact, even though I was working in a partnerships capacity, I came to believe that *all* service partnerships should originate within the customer success department.

Without customer success, you have no company. After all, the customer pays the bills.

At the time, chat and decision tree chatbots were hot. And Drift was pioneering these tools of Conversational Marketing, the category they'd named. I began by considering the services that partners could provide to their customers and the value our software would have for them. But my mentor Pete Caputa—the mastermind behind HubSpot's agency partner program, whom you met in a previous chapter—had a different take. It wasn't just about what our software could do for partner's customers. It was about what *we* could do for our partners. Customer value is the bare minimum; partner value raises the stakes and turns out to be both the most important and hardest part to nail.

Max Traylor, my favorite agency coach, called this the "Pirate Island problem." The problem with Pirate Island is that, in order to get there, you need to have already been there. In other words, if you want to take your partners to the place you want them to go, you have to have been there yourself.

When I approached Max about Pete's advice to focus on the partner value, he simply asked me, "Where are you taking your partners, and have you been there yourself?"

It hurt. The answer was no. Much like the CSM selling to a CMO, I hadn't been in their shoes with the software or personally achieved the outcomes we were touting. I hadn't sold or serviced the very things I thought our partners could do. Neither had our CS team. And our professional services teams at the time were doing very basic onboarding tasks—nowhere near enough customer value or impact to justify serious service dollars.

Discovering the true value of a partner comes from going to the place where you want your partners to go. That means, *doing the damn work yourself.* And if we're honest with ourselves, how else are we supposed to do this? We can't train and enable partners based on theory; we have to *show them* where they can go based on actual, real-world, tacit experience and tested services and methods. Think about it, without those, what are you asking your partners to do? I'll tell you—you're asking your partners, who aren't on your payroll, to spend a massive amount of time (and therefore money) figuring out the hardest problem in all of SaaS: **you're asking your partners to find the blueprint to your customer's success.**

Here's the reality check—if it were so easy, everyone would do it.

If we wanted to have our partners sell and evangelize conversational marketing services, we had to get to the dang island first.

Once again, I relied on my mentor, Pete Caputa, and his work with the CS organization at HubSpot. Pete came up with the HubSpot Inbound certification course that ended up training tens of thousands of people and partners globally. But HubSpot was already at scale—that mentorship gave me a North Star, but where did we start when we weren't even out of the starting gate? How was I supposed to make a dent now, not later?

That's where Max Traylor came in to help me solve the Pirate Island problem. In HubSpot's early days, Max created the intellectual property of "The Inbound Marketing Blueprint." The blueprint was the battle-tested methodology and step-by-step system (complete with template, presentations, worksheets, and state of work) for agencies to sell and service inbound marketing to the world. It was the answers to the test, not merely some product onboarding FAQs and how-tos. It was the map to the inbound Pirate Island.

The team and I spent months together with Max actually putting our hands on customer accounts—*doing* the work and *documenting* the journey. We were cartographers, mapping the uncharted waters of conversational marketing towards Pirate Island.

We developed a roadmap called "The Conversational Marketing Blueprint" to help agencies drive more leads with chat and manage the entire process from start to finish. While not a critical component of Drift's product, it was an essential resource for our customers. The blueprint encompassed various elements, such as "The Conversational Marketing Methodology," "The Conversational Marketing Maturity Model," and "The Conversational Framework (Engage, Understand, Recommend)." It also included templates for proposing services as an audit, for ongoing management, and other related tasks. This roadmap was not just a theoretical concept, but an actual map based on our successful implementation. When I say "we," I am referring to the partner team at Drift, not just the customer success team. We took the lead in driving customer success and partner value. Few things in my SaaS career have been as hard, but few things have made me as proud as that body of work. And the entire company rallied behind us.

Drift's VP of Marketing at the time was the aforementioned Mark Kilens, the same person who pioneered the whole category of inbound at HubSpot, in large part through the creation of HubSpot Academy. The HubSpot Academy was the ultimate partner-led experience. It involved partnering with customers, agencies, other SaaS businesses, and numerous departments within HubSpot to bring to life the leading training program for marketing, sales, and customer service/support.

Mark suggested turning the blueprint into a full conversational marketing course and certification not only for Drift partners, but our entire customer base and the market. Drift *Insider* was born—our version of HubSpot's Inbound Academy. Over a few months, we chose a few select partners—the most talented and respected marketing agencies in our ecosystem—to integrate Drift's conversational marketing technology with existing best practices in marketing automation and we were off to the races.

What were the results? Tens of thousands of people became conversational marketing certified, including Drift's own customer success team. In fact, it became mandatory for everyone. It generated better employees, better customers, better partners, and even generated new leads. If you were on LinkedIn at the time and paying attention to the social sphere in B2B martech, I can almost guarantee that you saw this as well. We were everywhere.

The massive windfall of customer success and partner value all came about because we didn't think we owned our customers—we knew we served them with our partners. We partnered up and transformed an entire industry, inspiring hundreds of copycats, and ultimately achieving a billion-dollar exit with a simple chatbot and a basic i-frame on a website.

It wasn't easy, but if you want to win in the Nearbound Era, you don't win with easy. You win with a passionate dedication to, as Drift CEO David Cancel said, "Putting the customer at the center of everything you do," as Pete Caputa said, "Solving for partner value first," and as Max said, "Documenting the path to Pirate Island yourself."

## The Power of Who: Building Your Ideal Partner Profile (IPP) for Nearbound Customer Success

At Drift, we identified Demand Gen and ABM agencies as our primary partners, starting with those with whom we already had close relationships and who had solid reputations in the industry with our best customers. We used those conversations to solidify a flywheel—training other partners along with our internal employees in the same services and best practices—resulting in the Conversational Marketing Blueprint, Drift Insider, and a partner and CS team that worked in tandem.

Best of all, by transitioning from a professional service organization to a customer/partner success organization, we resolved the common issue of "channel conflict" that often occurs within CS teams. In some cases, your internal employees might feel the urge to compete with a partner who provides similar services. If CS can instead focus on certifying that partner and involve them in the process, everyone can win. Your team levels up. They are now no longer just service providers but certified experts or even instructors and certifiers themselves.

I'll challenge conventional wisdom on this. Asking, "What is my ideal partner profile (IPP)?" is misleading. The nearbound customer success mindset begins by considering the people your customers are currently engaged with. Your IPP is someone who closely collaborates with your customers.

Your IPP is not a theoretical list of firmographics and qualifiers that make up an ideal partner universe. Instead, IPP is an enumerated list of actual partner accounts.

How do you create this list? Talk to customers. Ask them: "Who?"

We didn't choose the title for *Nearbound and the Rise of the Who Economy* by accident. The term "who" does not refer to a theory but rather to a list.

Who do your best customers already work with? It's not just a definition, it's a list. And you don't create that list by avoiding customers. You only create that list by talking to them, understanding them, and figuring out *who* surrounds them. Sure, you can have an IPP definition, but I see this far too often: a definition, but a complete lack of conversations, account names, and contact information. Partner people can fall into the trap of theory, not practice; they can fall into the trap of shipping reasons, not results.

Let me be clear, if you can't put W's on the board with the people and the partners your customers already trust, then you don't deserve a job.

Instead, abandon the ivory tower and engage with your organization. Identify your top customers and ask them the following questions:

- Who do they trust to assist in running their business unit (e.g., the departments/personas you service)?
- Who within their company is responsible for finding or managing relationships with other vendors, service providers, or contractors?
- Where do they seek help? Are there any events, thought leaders, influencers, or role models they admire or trust for assistance?
- Who else collaborates with them, and what outcomes are they delivering or promising?

As a partner manager, you should conduct interviews with those customers to identify their marketing agencies, system integrators (SIs), or service consultants, and determine who has the most tangential value for your organization. Throughout these interviews, build your lists.

Can you productize some kind of intellectual property into a service offering with your best partners? If so, you can create a training academy or certification with the right partners who already work with your best customers and then train or certify those existing service providers in your intellectual property. Mark the X of customer and partner value on the map and chart your course for your company and industry to Pirate Island. That's where the gold is.

## A Ride Along to Pirate Island

After launching productized services with clear pricing that impacts customers, your business dynamics shift. Salespeople may earn bonuses, professional services teams are motivated, and CFOs keep tabs on this new revenue.

The challenge is that just because you've developed these services and made them available, doesn't automatically mean that your partners are fully equipped to deliver them successfully to the end customers. There's a gap between offering these services and ensuring they genuinely meet customer needs effectively. Until your partners consistently demonstrate that they can make customers happy with these services, there will be a natural skepticism from your customer success and professional services (PS) teams towards each new partner's ability to deliver. This cautious stance is especially pronounced with new partners who haven't yet proven their capability in real-world customer scenarios.

At Drift, to address the challenge of ensuring our partners could effectively deliver our services, I introduced two key roles: the Partner Delivery Consultant (PDC) and the Partner Training Consultant (PTC). The PTC's mission was to train and certify new partners on our packaged services, preparing them to meet our standards for customer delivery. Certification meant partners had completed online training and successfully handled 3-5 deliveries with our customer success and professional services teams.

For example, the first delivery would be 100% led by the company, and the last delivery would be 100% led by the services partner. The second step would involve a 20% contribution from the partner and an 80% contribution from the software company. The third and fourth steps followed a similar pattern. By the end, your internal team was essentially just shadowing, and the partner was what we called "delivery certified."

Once certified, partners could independently manage their customer accounts, moving beyond initial training to actual service delivery, under supervision by the PDC.

Interestingly, these roles weren't placed within the partner team. With support from our CFO, the legendary Jim Kelliher, we embedded the PDC and PTC roles within the customer success and professional services organizations. This strategy aimed to bolster customer retention and success without inflating our operational expenses or COGS.

The "ride along" process was crucial for certification. This hands-on approach allowed partners to gradually take on more responsibility, starting with shadowing our team during initial deliveries and eventually leading the process themselves. This ensured that by the time partners were fully certified, they had practical experience and were ready to contribute to our customers' success.

As a leader in nearbound partnerships, once you get this flywheel spinning, you will have a reliable partner who can handle 25 out of your 100 forecasted implementations. Allow the CS leader to take credit for the implementations and customer impact instead of yourself. This is about making their CS business even more successful and ensuring that customers achieve greater success by leveraging the partner motion. The nearbound success model begins to revolve around these partnerships rather than solely relying on hiring new service employees. You didn't have to win the battle, but you still won the war.

CHAPTER 11

# SUCCESS THROUGH NEARBOUND PRODUCT
## (INTEGRATIONS, EXPERTS, AND MARKETPLACES)

In the two previous chapters, we've traced the evolution of customer success from a static state—a noun—to a dynamic process, a verb that embodies the continuous action of servicing. This transition reflects a fundamental shift in how SaaS businesses approach the retention and satisfaction of their customers. Now, we turn our focus to three creative nearbound approaches to servicing that overlap with the product strategy: integrations, expert communities, and marketplaces. Each plays a distinct but complementary role in creating a comprehensive support ecosystem without the need to expand an internal Professional Services Organization (PSO), which, while providing immediate support, often does so at the cost of the company's gross margins.

### Integrations

Getting integrations right is the best way to bolster your customer health and company success. In fact, for most SaaS companies, it's the highest leverage use of time for CS teams. There are some partner hills worth dying on. Integrations are one of them.

Remember: your software is just one small part of your customers' complex workflows. People, processes, and technologies are already in place for nearly every business initiative, including the infrastructure side, go-to-market side, and every other side. Facilitating the right integration makes your solution "stickier" and more valuable to that customer. The

ABM platform Rollworks found that customers with four or more integrations are 35% less likely to churn compared to those with just one integration enabled.

Your product must interoperate with customers' existing systems, and integrations provide the biggest clues about where CS teams should focus their energy.

When a CSM receives a new account from sales, they typically have a one-time task of determining which of the numerous integrations to set up with that customer. With a networked database like Reveal, a CSM can identify all integration partners (and their customers) and determine which integrations to set up.

In addition to this one-time task, you now need to manage thousands of pieces of technology scattered across your accounts. But how do you determine which integrations are the most important from the overwhelming array of options? The technology landscape is constantly evolving, with replacements, consolidations, and new solutions being introduced regularly.

For instance, Reveal might surface fresh intel that a customer has recently purchased another vendor's software but has not yet connected it through the integration you have with that vendor. This intelligence can trigger a conversation about what's changing in their world and how your product fits in. Don't you want to be aware of the business challenges and initiatives related to your product when an integration is available? The smart CSMs are already aware and take action on this information, not just once, but every time a piece of technology is integrated or disintegrated.

Reveal might also show you that a customer switched from one software provider to another. Or even earlier in the process, you may see one partner with a churn opportunity and another with an open new business opportunity. Exploring the reasons behind such a switch provides useful insights into evolving needs. You can pass those learnings on to your partners, making a "deposit in the trust fund" that starts a virtuous cycle of reciprocity.

Partners may return the favor by providing early warnings about potential customer churn risks to you. If another vendor is planning a major release that could disrupt your integration, your partner might hear about it first. Or they may learn that a client is switching tools or cutting the budget for your product area in their business unit. This real-time information sharing delivers a competitive advantage and strengthens your CS team's ability to proactively manage the benefits of their nearbound flywheel, not just at renewal time.

It's crucial to keep an eye on trends, such as when multiple customers start adopting a new product from a partner. This could indicate a market shift that, if acted upon quickly, can enhance customer retention.

The flip side of the new capabilities and demand for interoperability is the potential for new headaches and a never-ending stack of support tickets as your customers tap into an increasingly rich ecosystem of integration wants and needs. When onboarding a new client, prioritize the top integrations that align with their goals *right now*. Resist the temptation to connect every tool. Integration decisions should start with the customer's desired outcomes, not yours, even if that means embracing a competing tool or pushing the product team to build new integrations when a competitor to one of your top integrations starts earning more market share.

At Drift, I saw the value of cooperation over competition during the peak of the ABM Wars. Our early integrations for chat and ABM were with Clearbit and Demandbase—both amazing software vendors. Still, I helped 6sense sell into hundreds of Drift accounts because it was clear that if we wanted to serve our customers, we needed to do something special with 6sense too.

When our CSMs started seeing customers switching from incumbents to 6sense, we not only integrated with 6sense but also formed a "powered by" partnership with them. This partnership led to 6sense and Drift becoming two of the fastest growing Independent Software Vendors in history, making it one of the most successful ISV partnerships ever.

## iPaaS and Beyond

Not every integration needs to be productized. With the advent of iPaaS (Integration Platform as a Service), your tech team can now deliver basic integration features across a broader spectrum of tech partners more efficiently than ever, surpassing the capabilities of native app integrations. This isn't to say iPaaS solves all challenges, but it does offer real-time insights into potential integration opportunities through tools like Reveal's networked database. Generally, the larger the customer base and the associated Annual Recurring Revenue (ARR), the more you might consider developing native integrations. The bottom line is clear: in the Nearbound Era, customers demand seamless interoperability, and that's only achievable through thoughtful integrations.

Moreover, solution partners can craft even more tailored integrations to meet specific customer needs. Whether it's connecting to niche legacy systems for complex setups or introducing innovative features for new markets, these customized solutions are key to advancing the nearbound flywheel. When you notice opportunities in untapped markets, it's crucial to act decisively. Even with just a foundational open API, the right partners can extend your reach into new territories.

Putting wins on the board where no one else can is some of the sweetest fruit in partnerships. It's not easy pickings, but many rockstar careers in partnerships are born by knocking down the door to a new industry, vertical, or persona.

## Expert Communities

The vast range of integrations makes it impossible for vendors to understand every customer use case themselves and build the knowledge graph internally. Expert users are often able to explore niche applications for software that even developers don't expect. They also build authenticity and trust by helping customers without a sales agenda.

Companies like Zapier have figured out the advantage of deputizing these experts within an official community—serviced by the company's knowledge base, CS team, and nearbound partner ecosystem. As an integration platform connecting workflows across hundreds of apps, Zapier's internal team could never handle every customer use case. Instead, they created a network of certified automation consultants. These experts help users maximize Zapier through complex workflows and full business automation. Some even offer training to improve self-service skills.

While anyone can hire these consultants at market rates, many contribute free advice on Zapier's community forums. They build a reputation as top experts, aligning incentives with Zapier's mission of democratizing automation. By certifying and empowering these partners, Zapier treats them as an extension of their team. It becomes further momentum on their nearbound flywheel benefiting all parties.

This model is increasingly common among Web 3.0 firms, where engaged users often become more knowledgeable than the developers about emerging use cases.

Jasper.ai, an AI writing assistant company, cultivates a thriving expert user community—#JasperNation—on Facebook. Top users evolve into trusted, certified experts. These experts are usually the first people to comment when a user poses a never-before-asked question, like, "How do I write a compelling product description for Argyle sweaters in the voice of Dr. Seuss?"

You don't necessarily need to own these communities, either. Every profession in tech has its own informal, self-organizing online communities or "watering holes," as Jay McBain calls them, where buyers can call on experts they trust. You can build a community. Customers are seeking answers from people who've been to the places they want to go.

You can build these expert communities, or you can join them with your CS and partner teams. But whatever you do, don't ignore them.

## Marketplaces

Marketplaces are one of my favorite examples of network effects. As business models, they can be tricky, but as a *part* of your business model, a marketplace can drive customer value throughout the bowtie.

Even in the early days of PandaDoc where I served as the first Vice President of Sales & Partnerships all the way to our first 10,000 customers, templates and template marketplaces were a key part of our customer success and partner strategy. PandaDoc's template marketplace drove *the majority* of our new signup volume for our product-led growth funnel (in addition to helping customers reduce their time to value). We had community members, our best customers, and our partners create their favorite and most used templates into freely accessible documents anyone could download or add to their own PandaDoc accounts. Yes, there were certainly some SEO hacks we pulled off to garner some easy traffic in those days, but the point remained the same. Marketplaces are a force multiplier. PandaDoc made millions upon millions with this strategy, but never a penny directly from the marketplace itself. There was never any commerce, but the value for all parties was undeniable.

The visual SaaS platform, Miro, has nailed the template marketplace. Many of the visuals in this book began as templates. Not only do templates save users time, but also showcase utility by demonstrating possible use cases.

Notion—the platform the team and I used to write this book—has become a darling of the tech world by leveraging the power of both integrations and template marketplace. With over 80 native integrations (and well over 300 including 3rd party), Notion has become a popular knowledge base and all-in-one workspace. Many customers choose to build their entire back offices in Notion, replacing dozens of other tools with a single subscription.

These integrations make Notion especially sticky and help guarantee a certain amount of retention. But with this success comes the challenge of ensuring that Notion's more than 35 million users are getting continuous value, even as new features are added, and new use cases are discovered. Templates—prebuilt Notion pages that can be added to your workspace—have emerged as the first line of defense against the nagging feeling that the full potential of the software is not being realized.

After witnessing an explosion in independent template creation, Notion created an official template gallery where anyone can sell their templates with zero revenue share. Creators feel like they are a part of

Notion's community, and customers get help tailoring their Notion workspaces to their unique use cases.

One popular Notion creator, "Easlo," has grown a large following selling minimalist solutions designed to make life easier for busy people. "Every product is designed with a focus on elegance, simplicity, and ease," his website says.

In addition to templates, Easlo sells courses and tutorials on how to customize them. By conservative estimates, Easlo earns over $15k-$20k per month—and like PandaDoc, Notion foregoes all revenue sharing in favor of the free servicing that creators like Easlo provide their growing customer base. While some argue that Notion is leaving money on the table, the loyalty and exposure gained are worth more than any revenue share. Easlo's viral content on X and TikTok has brought countless millennials and Gen Z'ers into Notion's ecosystem. It's a perfect example of both network effects and the flywheel and proves that you don't need to monetize your marketplace to benefit.

Thomas Frank is another example of a partner/evangelist with no formal relationship to the company. Frank is a popular YouTuber who has attracted 3 million followers. He creates video walkthroughs and template tutorials with detailed instructions for other content creators who want to stay on top of their complex production schedules and workflows.

There are hundreds of other independent creators who specialize in making templates for lawyers, solopreneurs, engineers, and project managers. Notion's CS team would never have known in advance what templates a lawyer or YouTube creator needed because they've never solved those problems themselves. They couldn't service these niches nearly as well as the template creators who have been to their buyers' promised land and tested their solutions against real-world problems.

While Notion now offers an official consultant program, much of the template ecosystem grew organically from market incentives. Their former Head of Partnerships, Christina Cordova, implemented much of these learnings before taking them to First Round Capital as a Venture Partner, where she shaped investment in community-based models for customer success and GTM innovation. Notion's success is a case study in replacing hundreds of complex, headache-inducing decisions about how to service every possible niche with one strategic choice: empowering trusted influencers to do the servicing for them. I'll quote Jill again: *Your network is your net worth.*

## Bringing the Nearbound Success Flywheel Full Circle

It's common to see creators on Notion's template gallery featuring mock-up images of slick software boxes, complete with the trademark sheen of a plastic wrapper. Even though the products are delivered digitally (through a link to a template, not even a file), it evokes a nostalgic longing for simpler times—tearing open the box, flipping through instructions, and waiting to unlock some new superpower as soon as the progress bar hits 100%.

This is what software is all about, simplifying solutions linked to customer outcomes. With all the sophisticated new tools and integrations available, it's easy to forget that software is supposed to make our lives easier, not harder.

In the subscription world, packaging has changed, and with it, the process of guaranteeing your customer's success. This process begins with the humble recognition that you and your team will never have all the answers. However, once you realize this, you're liberated to provide so much more value—working with partners who know your customers' needs, surround them, and are eager to work with you to serve them better.

The nearbound revolution isn't coming for you or your CS team's jobs. Instead, it's putting a premium on the services you provide customers and urging you to prioritize decisions that help the customer win.

The advice from my old boss David Cancel—to put the customer at the center of everything you do—has never been more important as a first principle. Surround them with integrations, expert communities, trusted marketplaces, and network effects, and you will create a world where everyone can win together.

# Part 6
## The Nearbound Overlay

*"Nearbound is transcending traditional boundaries and redefining modern GTM. For B2B Chief Revenue Officers and sales leaders, embracing this approach is not just an opportunity; it's a strategic imperative.*

*This isn't a "Partnerships thing." It's a calculated GTM maneuver designed to max out partner-sourced revenue and NRR through the power of trusted relationships, unified GTM (co-market/co-sell), and tightly aligned collaboration (planning and execution)*

*Those who adopt Nearbound swiftly will not merely outpace their competition, they will redefine the battleground in the categories they serve. Step #1 is to acknowledge this fact: just because you have a partner program doesn't mean you have a nearbound program."*

— Alex J. Buckles, 5x Founder & Head of Product, Partnerships, and Value Engineering at Forecastable

## CHAPTER 12

# NEARBOUND PARTNERSHIPS

Partnerships departments have a bad rap with other GTM teams. If you ask CROs and sellers what they think of partnerships, more often than not, you'll hear some version of the following:

> "They only attach themselves to deals that are already closing."

> "Why would I complicate my deals with more people?"

> "It's not clear what the actual ROI on partnerships is?"
> "It doesn't seem worth the investment."

So long as partnerships operates on their own lonely island, not taking ownership of their company's GTM activities, and not helping where they can, these beliefs will continue. And so long as partnerships is a department, rather than a strategy for every department, this misalignment will persist. I dive deeper into the leadership required to inculcate a nearbound culture in the final chapter entitled, *The Nearbound Mindset*.

When partnerships is a strategy for every department instead of a silo, it's what I've referred to earlier in this book as an "overlay model." An overlay model is what allows marketing, sales, success, and product to run nearbound plays and embed partner motions in the fabric of the company. To make the overlay work, one thing is critical: the partner team working hand-in-glove with the operations team, and then executing in the same fashion with their other GTM teams. And that happens when a leader with *a nearbound mindset* makes it happen. This closing section on partnerships, ops, rhythm of the business, and mindset is how the previous sections all come to life at your company.

An overlay model doesn't mean you don't need a partnerships department. You will need someone to do the work required to find, build, and nurture those partnerships in the first place. But don't stop there. The overlay model is all about who, and on which teams, you overlay the partnering motions with, and who you're surrounding your customers with.

Once you find, activate, and nurture good partnerships, you can overlay them and start driving revenue together with ops and each department. So how do you go about finding, activating, and nurturing those partner relationships in the first place?

## Finding Nearbound Partnerships in an Overlay Model

Probably the meanest I get when talking to partnerships or GTM crowds is when I talk about "finding" new partners. Here I must reference the section in the *Nearbound Customer Success* chapter, "The Power of Who, Building Your Ideal Partner Profile (IPP) for Nearbound Customer Success":

> Your IPP is not a theoretical list of firmographics and qualifiers that make up an ideal partner universe. Instead, IPP is an enumerated list of actual partner accounts.
>
> How do you create this list? Talk to customers. Ask them: "Who?"

Why would this sentiment evoke the meanest side of me? Because, as I've said, if you can't put W's on the board with the companies your customers already work with, you don't have a job, period. In the nearbound-surround model—where you are trying to overlay partnerships against each department—you have to start with the customer and talk to them. Build the dang list of *who* your best customers already work with. Start there and stay there for as long as you can.

I can certainly hear the objection:

> "But Jared, we're going up-market, or expanding into a new territory, we don't have customers where we are trying to grow."

Well, I'll be just as direct with my next piece of advice. Talk to the dang customers you want and figure out who they are already doing business with, where they live, who they listen to, and who they trust. Partner leaders need to be experts on not just the partner, but ultimately the market and the customer, even if those lines blur, grow, or change.

You have a list of target accounts. Your list of target partners needs to be based on the nearbound network of the customers you have and the customers you want. And there is no better way (in addition to connecting with your customers on Reveal) to get those lists than through conversations.

Of course, you have your sales and success organizations on the phones all the time too. They are having the majority of conversations with your customers and the ones you want. Leverage them. It's actually easier than you think. Take, for instance, call recording software and sales intelligence platforms like Gong or Clari. Obviously, the data on these platforms is only as good as the conversations and questions happening therein. But there's a trick every great partner pro needs to implement right away. And it's simple: **Get commitment from your sales and CS teams to ask simple questions.**

Questions like:

- What (service) partners are you working with today, helping on related initiatives?
- What technologies are important to our discussions today from an integration, platform, or workflow perspective?

There are plentiful permutations to the above questions but ensuring they are asked is critical for my favorite modern partner hack: call recording tags and filters.

Every day (or at minimum weekly) someone in your partner org should be looking at the specific names—the who—that your potential and actual customers are bringing up on calls.

I'll give you a specific example. While at Drift, I had an alliances manager, Justin Bartels, who was one of the best front-line alliance managers I have ever seen. For the OG PartnerHackers, you might recognize the name, as he co-hosted a few dozen episodes of the podcast *PartnerUp* with me before Isaac and I launched PartnerHacker and ultimately rebranded to nearbound.com.

Justin was dang good, and he needed to be. He had a $6M annual quota (not a typo—this was a massive stretch) and hit $5M of it. Justin owned the frontline relationship with Marketo and Adobe, our largest alliance partner. So, what did Justin do? Justin had a flag for any time "Marketo" or "Adobe" was mentioned in a call. Not only did he use that to drive his own nearbound plays—connecting our AEs and AMs with their counterparts at Adobe—he also used it to identify combinations with the words "agency," "consultant," or "systems integrator," (SI or GSI). Those were our best partner leads.

Think about it. I'm sure you've tried to go "outbound" to recruit new partners. And I'm sure you've tried using phrases like, "This isn't a sales email, I just want to explore partnership opportunities."

You and everyone else, including the SDRs who have co-opted the word "partnership" to mean "cold sale" in outbound messaging. Those DMs and emails don't work like they used to. But guess what does work? Pinging an agency partner and mentioning a couple of their clients who have recently become customers of yours. That's what Justin did with the solution partner program at Drift. He'd flag those names and inform our partner managers. Those managers would be able to triangulate the relationships in our funnel, customer base, and calls. Partner managers would then be able to get intel, influence, or intros from those very prospects, customers, or even other partners like Adobe themselves.

When it comes to finding and recruiting new partners, customers are still the answer. And it turns out that nearbound plays work just as well, if not even better, on partner recruitment. Surround the partners you want with the customers, prospects, and other partners to show them you know them and demonstrate maximum relevance.

Live in the market, understand the customer, and get your customer teams to do this as well. That's the best way to demystify partner recruitment from a vague definition of firmographics to an actual list of partner accounts. Better yet, when you truly align customer teams to asking even one or a couple of simple questions, this isn't some data scraping exercise: instead, it's a constantly renewing flywheel of new partner conversations that come in daily.

Yes, there are plenty of nuances to partner recruitment, contracts, program building, tiering, and incentives. Luckily, with industry media companies and communities like Partnership Leaders, nearbound.com, and others emerging, there are tons of resources in the market to help you. Find and use them, but don't forget that the best way to recruit partners is through talking to the market.

Here are some best practices for finding and approaching partners:

- (Dis)qualify partners using what Bernhard Friedrichs and Martin Scholz, Founders of PartnerXperience, call the 4 C's methodology:
    - **Customer base:** Does your potential partner have a relevant and accessible customer base that matches your company's ICP?
    - **Credibility:** Do they have the credibility to represent your products or services to the customer?

- ○ **Capability:** Does the potential partner have the models, systems, and/or technology capabilities to execute?
  - ○ **Commitment:** Are they committed to the partnership and the mutual goals created together?
- Ben Wright, Founder of Partner Fuel, leverages an ecosystem like HubSpot that he knows is connected to his target account list. He then uses LinkedIn's Sales Navigator to find target contacts (ideally the Director of Partnerships, Owner, or Revenue Officer). Once he's found some names, he'll use a tool like Apollo.ai to get the contact info. He then sends a succinct message explaining why he's reaching out, including a value statement, or what he'd like to give them through the partnership.
- Use tools like Reveal and Salesforce together to create tags and automatic campaigns based on customer data to help find partners linked to your target accounts. Aaron Howerton, Sr. Program Manager, Partner Ops & Experience at Samara, creates custom objects in Salesforce for "Partner Prospects" alongside target lists so that he is notified of partners that he should be going after.

## Activating Partner Value & the First Helper Advantage

My business partner and CMO at Reveal, Isaac Morehouse talks frequently about "social capital." The thing about social capital is it must be accumulated before it can be spent. It's logic, not magic. But, yet again, simple doesn't mean easy. To activate partnerships, you must always be replenishing your "trust fund" with deposits that your sales and marketing teammates can withdraw against to run the most powerful plays in the GTM playbook. With partnerships, the mantra "help first," hearkens back to the Golden Rule:

Do unto others as you would have them do unto you.

Helping others reach their promised land doesn't guarantee others will help you in kind. But failing to consider your partners' needs first has long-term consequences that can stymie your early successes. As discussed in the *Nearbound Customer Success* section, understanding your partner value is critical. Not what's in it for you even your joint customers, but what's in it for the partners.

"Helping first" is an important distinction over "giving first." You can *give* all sorts of stuff that people don't care about. For example, try gifting a bottle of wine to someone who doesn't drink. Remember, *trust comes from helping people reach their promised land.* That means you must understand what exactly your partner's promised land is and how you can help them get there.

The term "partner activation" gets thrown around a lot in our industry. This partner lifecycle phase is about ensuring that your partners are trained and enabled enough to give your customers first-class service. But it's also about solidifying yourself and your company as the partner you promised you'd be. I see *so many* partner managers get it wrong here. At the risk of sounding like a broken record, I'll say it again: if you don't get W's on the board for your sales team, you'll be out of a job, but if you don't get W's on the board for your partner early, you'll lose them.

Jeremy Seltzer, CRO at Movable Ink once told me, "I want to produce a ton from my partner ecosystem, which means we have to help our partners a whole heck of a lot."

That's the difference between a junior varsity player and a pro. A pro understands that if they want to make a ton of money, they had better help others do the same.

At the same time that you're getting new partners trained and ready to storm the hill, you need to be plucking the low-hanging fruit that aligns with the goals you discussed with them during the prospecting phase. Use Reveal or other account mapping tools to see the customers of yours who are prospects of theirs and get them in a room together. Help them close a deal before they even step foot in your customer arena. This will set a precedent for your relationship. It will tell them that you're serious about helping them get to their promised land, and it will motivate them to do the same for you.

Partner incentives are vital during the activation phase. Here are some ways Gwyn Edwards, Director of Partnerships & Alliances at Zift Solutions, has activated partners:

- **Money:** Discounts, margins, gift cards, rebates, SPIFFs, and bonuses are all effective methods of grabbing your partners' attention.
- **Leads:** For the right partner, supporting them with a BDR can also move the needle.
- **Co-marketing and co-selling:** You can get mindshare by offering partners proactive support with marketing and sales over and above the enablement tools you provide.
- **Tiers:** Some businesses like to incorporate tiered rewards such as the "bronze, silver, gold" medal system. Offering some way for partners to earn more rewards or points for completing behaviors can make a huge difference in partner engagement.

- **Awards:** Awards like Partner of the Year or President's Club can be powerful incentives for partners motivated by the achievement or associated status.
- **Contests:** Gamification through contests or sales leaderboards also can drive results by tapping into partners' competitive spirits.

## Nurturing: Becoming a Partner-Centric Organization

If you apply the principles of this book consistently, your sales and marketing teams will soon be hooked on running nearbound plays. They'll finally start to respect partnerships for enabling their success.

But with this new power comes the responsibility to deliver repeated results.

What if your partners start withdrawing too much trust without putting enough deposits back into the fund? Suddenly, your teammates are pounding on your door demanding more intel, influence, and intros from partners. Yet your trust reserves are running low. Partners wonder why they should start, much less keep, helping when you've done next to nothing for them.

Transitioning to a partner-centric organization requires more than lip service. It requires putting partners first across the business. When Nadella from Microsoft, Benioff from Salesforce, or Rangan from HubSpot talk about partner centricity, they mean it.

Whether you call it a partner-first or help-first mentality, the principle is the same: focus on fast-tracking partner time-to-value before you try to cash in social capital you don't have. That's why I believe many, if not most, partnerships should emanate from the customer success department. If you can't help your partners put their own W's on the board with the customers you already have, how can you expect either side to risk it with new business opportunities and the pressure of the CRO and sales funnel? You can try, but I've yet to see an industry giant emerge with that partner culture.

You've heard of the first-mover advantage; in the Nearbound Era, there is a distinct first-helper advantage. The first-helper advantage is rooted in one of the core principles of influence outlined by renowned bestselling author and psychologist Robert Cialdini—the rule of reciprocity. Humans feel an instinctive urge to return favors when someone helps them first. It's embedded in our nature.

No doubt this was essential for group survival, as well as inter-group cooperation when people lived in small tribes. But while some people view business through the lens of warlike metaphors around cutthroat competition, we're moving back to the time when cooperation will determine who survives and who perishes.

Most people, Cialdini says, get it backward. They think reciprocity means that if you will do something for us, then we will do something for you. Grokking the first-helper advantage involves a certain amount of conviction and proof that it works until you internalize and operationalize the logic of repeated games.

In a game with just one round, it might make economic sense to try to extract as much from your partner as you can. But with repeat rounds, a different dynamic emerges. More complex business ecosystems can only operate when trust flows freely through the system—lubricating the gears, reducing frictions, and feeding the momentum of your partnership flywheels. Reciprocity is made for these kinds of long-term games. It is more likely to verge on manipulation if there is just one transaction and the social capital runs dry. Remember, trust is gained in drops and lost in buckets.

For example, picture a middle-aged man with a cheesy mustache and cheap suit knocking on your door one summer afternoon. He offers to give you a free rotating fan just for listening to his spiel. You weren't planning to buy an air conditioner. But now you feel compelled to hear him out. The salesman drones on about AC specs you don't understand as you both stand sweating in the heat. As he spews hot air, the cool air from your perfectly good air-conditioning unit billows out your door.

In this case, Cialdini says we are justified in accepting the gift and then immediately shutting the door in the salesman's face. He tried to manufacture false reciprocity through slick manipulation. We shouldn't, and typically don't, reward such behavior. It's not helpful to either party. If this is what our attempt at wooing partners looks like—little more than a glorified bribe—we shouldn't expect them to reciprocate.

It's crucial to distinguish this manipulative approach from authentic reciprocity which benefits both parties over a longer time horizon. If you only help partners as a way to leverage their sense of obligation and get something in return, you will breed distrust and truncate your partnership before it ever matures.

Again, the Golden Rule remains the compass. Treat others as you would want to be treated. Help others how you would want to be helped.

For the most part, this means building partnerships rooted in their goals, not around creating artificial indebtedness.

When you genuinely care about your partner's success, you tap into the true persuasive power of reciprocity.

Here are some ways to reap the First-Helper Advantage:

- **Share valuable intel:** Provide partners with insights, contacts, and info to help them close more deals and save time. Pair every ask for a nearbound "I" of intel, influence, or intro with a give of the same.
- **Spotlight partners publicly:** Celebrate partners in newsletters, on social media, in blog posts, at events, and in external messaging.
- **Offer exclusive access:** Give partners early previews, betas, and insider access to your product roadmap.
- **Resolve issues quickly:** Provide dedicated support contacts and expedited processes to fix partner problems faster.
- **Co-develop integrations:** Build custom integrations, connectors, and packages tailored to partners' needs.
- **Onboard thoughtfully:** Take time to welcome and train new partner team members at all levels.
- **Collaborate on campaigns:** Involve partners early in planning marketing campaigns, launches, and events.
- **Recognize excellence:** Call out and reward partners who drive major deals, boost pipeline, or deliver exceptional work.

Now that you're recruiting, activating, and nurturing partners, it's time to align with ops and make sure the right data and processes are flowing so you can overlay nearbound into every department.

## CHAPTER 13
# NEARBOUND OPERATIONS

If the goal of nearbound is to overlay the partnerships motion onto every department, there is no better counterpart and partner in this initiative than the operations team. Whether they go by "sales operations," "business operations," or "revenue operations," the core function is the same: to exploit the data, technologies, and processes to measure and accelerate the business toward its core metrics and objectives.

In short, to drive nearbound revenue, you need to get your attribution and compensation models right and ensure partner-relevant data is flowing to the right places. The power of a networked database with partners will go untapped if you're not deliberate about it. Ops is where you'll get it done.

The explosion of information technologies, longer sales cycles, more complex contractual agreements, and a whole lot more data across every department have made ops more important. The operations department must function like the conductor of an orchestra, ensuring that different departments are harmonized in their goals and strategies. The abundance of information provided by new tools is crucial for determining what's working and what isn't. But this deluge of data makes it easy to overlook the fact that businesses, like orchestras, are made up of people. Ops departments always face the danger of losing their soul in a sea of spreadsheets.

It's too easy to develop a top-down view that is disconnected from ground realities. The COO and CFO tweak formulas and plot linear journeys that cascade down the demand waterfall. With each hand-off, a few more leads get pruned or leak out the bottom. The reality rarely meets the model, and targets are missed.

When this happens, few stop to question the operating model itself. Instead, they point fingers. Marketing blames sales for not closing. Sales blames marketing for poor quality leads. Everyone blames the CRM, and clamors for more dashboards, automation, and reporting.

Why is this happening?

In part, it's because the traditional "waterfall model" that has been the mainstay of many operational strategies no longer captures the nuanced, non-linear buyer journeys of today's customers. Leads don't march uniformly down a predefined path. Analyzing a linear pipeline is insufficient to diagnose and fix leakage. We need to redraw our maps.

The fact that many voices surround buyers through their nonlinear journey—some of them your partners—means we have a chance to improve the ops function and get it closer to reality by getting closer to partnerships.

## The Hard Problem of Attribution

In many organizations, conflicts around attribution have long simmered beneath the surface. As multiple departments—sales, marketing, customer success—and external entities like partners play integral roles in the customer journey, a tug-of-war ensues over who gets credit for a lead's conversion or a deal's closure. The CRM ecosystem—the territory where these battles are waged—becomes a contested space. Different teams stake their claims, promoting their preferred metrics as the primary drivers of success.

Adding more data to the conversation can just add fuel to the fire. Let's say marketing is focused on metrics like click-through rates (CTR) from a targeted campaign. This CTR could indicate initial interest, leading them to believe their campaign was the primary driver for subsequent conversions. Meanwhile, sales might point to lead response time and the number of touchpoints before a sale, arguing that it was their timely intervention or a specific sales pitch that sealed the deal.

Adding to the complexity, the rise of partnership programs has introduced another layer to this tug-of-war. A partnerships team might be tracking UTM parameters to assess which partner referrals are converting. Now, armed with their influence data, they want to claim credit, given potential commissions at stake for them and the partners they recruited. But if a lead first clicked a partner link but only converted after a direct sales call following a marketing email, the waters of attribution get even murkier.

What's worse is that many leaders aren't as concerned about the ops side of partnerships as they are about the revenue they generate. Ironically, the same leaders—many of whom come from sales backgrounds—understand the importance of ops in other GTM departments, but somehow put blinders on when considering partnerships. This is a mistake; instead of supposedly saving resources by not allowing them to get the tech to succeed, they waste it by hiring partner pros with one hand tied behind their back.

Latané Conant, CRO at 6sense, says of partnership ops:

> "There's only so much you can do throwing partner managers around. They can be wildly inefficient if you don't have the structure set up to make them successful. It's not about the size of your partner team, it's about your infrastructure. I wouldn't hire a bunch of people if you're not willing to set the infrastructure up."

Enter Revenue Operations (RevOps)—an attempt to bridge these divides. In recent years, RevOps has begun to consolidate the functions of sales, marketing, and CS ops into a unified entity. This convergence aims to align strategies and metrics, effectively reducing territorial skirmishes within the CRM. By fostering a shared responsibility for the entire customer lifecycle, RevOps promotes holistic thinking over departmental silos. The intent is clear: create a seamless flow of information and collaboration, such that the question isn't who gets credit, but rather, how the collective enterprise can best serve the customer and drive revenue growth.

The consolidation under RevOps is a step in the right direction. But this is just the beginning of the ongoing evolution of nearbound operations.

As we transition from the How Economy which emphasizes processes and methods, to the Who Economy which centers on relationships and human interactions, our traditional metrics are due for an overhaul. With its integrated reach across all departments, ops is uniquely positioned to champion and navigate this evolution. Ops must act as the neural network of an organization—ensuring that information from one end reaches all other relevant parts, finishing the job of breaking down the old silos and zero-sum competitive struggles. The goal should be a cohesive enterprise where every department and partner orbits around the shared mission of customer-centric growth.

## Channel Conflict at HubSpot: A Case of Attribution Tensions

A good example of the hard problem of attribution and channel conflict comes from HubSpot, in the early days of their channel partnerships with marketing agencies all the way through the present. In theory, such channel partnerships should have created a win-win scenario. But

HubSpot's early operating model set the stage for a turf war between their partners and sales teams.

Pete Caputa, whom I credit with coming up with the partnerships overlay thesis, notes that HubSpot still has yet to adopt a full overlay model. Instead, he says, they have been "half pregnant" with an overlay for quite some time.

Recall from the earlier chapters that Pete was an early leader at HubSpot—the architect of its agency partner program.

Here's how he described the problem:

> "When we started the channel program it was completely separate... [P]artners could register leads and that would block the direct sales team from pursuing them. They were also blocked from getting credit for deals that were in the direct sales team's names. There were limits to the number of leads that could be in both a direct rep's name and a partner's name."

As the program got bigger, the conflict grew.

"That was an awful system," Pete recalls.

HubSpot's operational decision to wall off certain leads to specific teams or partners meant that at any given time, two arms of the organization were likely to be working at cross-purposes.

Seeking a remedy, they shifted to a model where both parties—direct sales and partners—could receive partial credit for a sale under stipulated conditions. But instead of making everyone happy, Pete notes, it just pissed everyone off.

While double compensation can function as a Band-Aid, this whole problem could have been avoided if they had baked partnerships-as-overlay into their operating model rather than partnerships as a distinct silo.

This tale of operational misalignment is not unique to HubSpot. Trillions of dollars are being wasted in B2B software every year. Everyone hates the meetings where people representing different teams fight over credit. After grappling with these issues for years, HubSpot has finally decided to transition to a full overlay model. In this approach, partners will work in tandem with direct reps on deals, while the partner manager's role will pivot to nurturing the broader relationship. The bitter competition over attribution underscores the need for a more nuanced approach to allocating credit for deals won.

Next, we'll delve into the practicalities: the tactics, metrics, tools, technologies, and rhythms that ops teams can employ to accelerate the transition into the Nearbound Era, where departments are aligned both internally with each other and externally with partners.

## Partner Attach: The North Star Metric

The "partner attach" rate has emerged as one of the most important metrics for organizations adopting a nearbound strategy. For ops teams, it can function as the Holy Grail, the North Star, and the single metric that matters most—if it is worked into the operating model correctly. At its core, the partner attach rate simply measures whether a partner was involved in or influenced a particular deal. It can refer to the engagement of channel partners, agencies, resellers, or technology partners that are attached to a deal or customer account. This can encompass co-marketing, integrated technologies, referral relationships, or various other forms of strategic alliance.

Before I continue, I'll address the protests I know are coming now to get them out of the way. No, partner-sourced revenue is not a better metric. And no, partner-sourced isn't as important to follow as partner attach. Why? Because as I explained before, gone are the days of leads marching through the doors of your pipeline like ants headed to a picnic. In the same interview with Latané, she echoed this sentiment in her advice to partner managers:

> "Sourced pipeline is the absolute worst metric to use. Because no one really sources a deal ever—marketing doesn't source it, sales doesn't source it. Don't fall into the marketing losing game of attribution. Look at partner attach rate in the customer base. That's what we track. It'll help you build your ecosystem."

Partner attach is a simple yes/no metric regarding partner contribution: was there a partner involved in this deal? This simplicity is one of its greatest strengths. Unlike convoluted multi-touch attribution models, the partner attach rate cuts through the noise to provide a clear directional signal.

From here, the ops team can then track a variety of more complex metrics and key performance indicators for each cohort such as:

- Win rates
- Average deal size
- Customer retention
- Expandability/upsell potential

This same simplicity, however, also opens the idea of partner attach up to criticism. I've been fought on this point numerous times while speaking at events. The reaction is often visceral. People say that partner attach itself doesn't accomplish anything—you can attach a partner to anything without seeing results. And they are right. But in almost every case, deals with partner attach outperform across these KPIs compared to non-attached deals.

The more sophisticated argument levied against partner attach has been voiced best by Sunir Shah, CEO of AppBind. Sunir says that we still have to assess whether partners are contributing real value or not, or whether they are riding your coattails.

The key distinction is what TEN70 Co-Founder and partnerships veteran Aaron McGarry calls "value-driven attach." This means establishing clear criteria and requirements for what constitutes a value-added attachment. Randomly slapping partners onto deals doesn't cut it. There must be demonstrated value.

For example, valid partner attachments could include:

- Joint selling engagement that directly impacted deal progress
- Qualified referrals that convert to pipeline
- Technical integrations that expanded product value
- Strategic input that shaped the planning process

The litmus test is, "Did this partner's involvement substantially improve our chances of winning the deal?"

If yes, that merits an attach. If not, it should not be arbitrarily counted. It is important for leadership to define partner attach with ops with little to no ambiguity. This will be especially important when you begin to compare the performance of your partner-attached deals. This is where the true power of tracking partner attach emerges.

## The Power of Comparative Analysis

By segmenting performance metrics by these two cohorts—attached and non-attached deals—the impact of partner involvement becomes measurable and actionable. I am not suggesting that ops should do away with other metrics or attribution models, but rather that it should overlay partner attach across these other metrics.

For example, consider a scenario where there are 200 accounts up for renewal in the customer success department during a given quarter. The goal is to retain 195 of these accounts. If partners are involved in 55 of these renewals, and all 55 of them are likely to renew, this is a significant signal that should be included in the reporting.

Ops can examine marketing campaign conversion rates for efforts with partner co-promotion versus those without. Or, it can analyze sales cycle length for attached deals against non-attached. Surfacing these partner metrics and reporting them upwards at appropriate intervals—weekly, monthly, quarterly, and annually—becomes a core responsibility of a nearbound operations team.

I'll reiterate that, in almost every scenario, the partner-attached cohort will outperform. Analyzing the magnitude of the benefit from partner attach then empowers teams to pinpoint which partnerships to double down on, and provides proof of the value these partners are bringing—allowing for further investment in the relationship.

Which campaigns drive the highest attach rates and corresponding conversion lift?

For which products/segments is our value proposition strengthened most by partners?

Which partners influence which metrics?

Sophisticated teams are already overlaying partner metrics into their operational workflows. For example, they might use a sales or revenue intelligence platform like Gong or Clari to analyze the breakdown of the pipeline, scoring leads and deals based on various activity metrics, including levels of partner involvement. If a partner is not involved, that's a surface-level risk—a vital signal.

But operations isn't just about gathering this data; it's about making it actionable. During the weekly forecast meeting, someone from ops should be bringing this risk to the salesperson's attention and providing them with intel about which partners might already have this opportunity as a customer. If three partners are associated with an opportunity, yet none have been approached to help close the deal, this provides an immediate action point for the sales rep (see *The Nearbound Sales Blueprint* for a refresher course on how to accomplish this).

Win rates are one of the best metrics your team can improve by working with partners—don't ignore them at the finish line. In fact, this can often be the best opportunity for bringing partners in, since the ask of the partner is small, yet can send a powerful signal of trust to the account to move forward with a purchase.

Once again, thanks to technology like Reveal, these workflows can be built directly on top of the CRM. But it's not enough to react to data when it surfaces at risk deals; operations must be proactively establishing certain rhythms, recurring tasks, and incentives to reflect the importance of partner attach throughout all departments. As ops begins to reveal the significance of partnerships and the immediate comparative value they bring, the next step is for company leadership to incorporate these insights into the operationalization of a collaborative nearbound culture.

## Culture & Cadence: What You Promote, What You Tolerate

The most fundamental task of operations is the creation and nurturing of company culture. Culture doesn't stem from vapid slogans and motivational posters plastered on office wall, but from the cadences and rituals that surface the right information for the right people at the right time. The rhythm of business, established by ops, is what determines which behaviors are rewarded versus neglected.

Let's start with the first principle of culture: **incentives matter**. As my former CEO David Cancel of Drift defines it, "Culture is what you promote and what you tolerate."

Or, as basic economics teaches, if you want more of something, subsidize it. Want less? Tax it.

Top-performing companies haven't smashed through their revenue goals quarter after quarter just by scrutinizing spreadsheets. Rather, they've simplified operations by improving culture—starting by aligning incentives. Aligning incentives starts by setting concrete goals and clear expectations reflected in daily standups, weekly reviews, monthly planning meetings, quarterly business reviews, and annual compensation planning.

Day-in-the-life reporting is where incorporating partner metrics is essential. Pull partner data into the regular meetings and rhythms of each department. We'll get into how to do this step by step in the next chapter.

Managers and leadership alike should be looking to integrate partner metrics not only into their management and reporting cadences but also in compensation plans. Here are a few ways you can do this:

1. **Annual Target Qualifier:** Institute an annual target qualifier, for example, and make it mandatory for salespeople to achieve over a 50% partner attach rate to meet their annual quotas. This can ensure constant collaboration with partners throughout the year. Such a qualifier could also serve as a prerequisite to earning exclusive recognitions like the "President's Club."
2. **Accelerators Contingent on Partner Attach Rate:** Provide accelerators, additional earnings, or bonuses to salespeople when they exceed their targets. This can be tied to the partner attach rate. Make it a prerequisite to hit that 50% partner attach rate to qualify for these earnings.
3. **Quota Retirement:** Even if partners receive commissions for their contribution, credit salespeople with the full deal value towards their annual sales quota. This ensures that salespeople

are not penalized for collaborating with partners and emphasizes the value of the partnership.
4. **Standard Pro-serve Rate:** Finally, eliminate potential conflicts of interest and streamline compensation. Even if a service partner is delivering the services, the organization should pay its standard professional service rate.

Measure, commit to the effort, and, when greatness shows, reward it.

## Case Study: Acquia's Shift to Partner-Centric Compensation

Acquia, a leading cloud platform for building, delivering, and optimizing digital experiences, is a prime example of the significance of fostering alignment between internal teams and external partners. Like many organizations, Acquia faced the challenge of aligning their account executives with core partners. While both parties thrived individually, they struggled to work together effectively. Despite this, there was a realization that partners needed to be involved because the metrics were too good to ignore. This realization was cemented by the ops department, which, through meticulous tracking at the CRM level, confirmed the superior performance metrics when sales and partnerships collaborated.

Quarterly business reviews (QBRs) consistently showcased better win rates, larger deal sizes, and faster deal closures when partners were actively involved compared to other metrics. Leadership at Acquia recognized that achieving their desired goals required more than just encouraging account executives to work with partners.

The pivotal moment was when Acquia decided to intertwine partnership involvement with compensation. They mandated that to qualify for the esteemed President's Club, account executives needed to source 50% of their revenue from partnerships. While the account executives were compensated for all deals, only the revenue that involved partners counted towards their annual quota. This shift in incentives transformed behavior. Involving partners in deals went from being an option to a natural inclination for account executives.

This is how operations can harmonize people and data, and align short and long-term objectives. Acquia solved their problem by updating their maps—changing their operating model—in light of new information about the terrain.

Returning to our musical metaphor, operations must embrace its central place as the orchestra's conductor. This isn't about keeping strict time, like a metronome, but rather orchestrating harmony among various sections—ensuring that the brass, strings, and percussion resonate in a musical masterpiece. Harmony goes beyond merely following a metronomic beat—it's about dynamic adaptation, where each section responds to the others in real time.

The heart of operations lies in its ability to bridge the immediate with the future and align the daily grind with the strategic horizon. While tools and tech are indispensable, they are merely instruments. The real melody emerges when these tools are tuned to the core rhythm of the business and the market.

It's not about being led by the data but leading with it. Running a business, like conducting an orchestra, demands nuance. So, while operations can lay down the foundational notes with data, the true art lies in interpreting, adjusting, and innovating, ensuring that every department plays its part and does so in harmony with the whole.

So, you've got the right metrics and data flowing to the right places, and compensation and credit are properly aligned to include partners. Now you can get serious about overlaying nearbound onto every department. But what does that actually look like day to day, week to week, month to month, quarter to quarter, and year to year?

Let's dive into the rhythm of the business and see.

## CHAPTER 14

# NEARBOUND & THE RHYTHM OF BUSINESS

You've heard phrases like, "Whether or not you define your culture, you have one." Or "Culture eats strategy for breakfast." Or, as Ben Horowitz put it, "What you do is who you are."

Of all the Silicon Valley speak, culture is, and has always been, a primary objective of the CEOs and founders I've seen create category-defining companies.

I've seen good culture, I've seen bad culture, and I've seen emergent culture. I've been a change agent for culture as well as a passenger to it. Here's what I can say: I'd much rather be in charge of my company culture than have my culture be in charge of my company. But how to do it?

Remember how my boss and the CEO of Drift, David Cancel, defined culture as "what you promote and what you tolerate?"

Well, that was only half the definition.

The second half is *the cadences and rituals to enforce them.* At the time (2018-ish), Drift was one of the fastest-growing SaaS companies in a space that was replete with competitors—website chat. What I saw DC do at Drift was so simple and so powerful it changed how I thought about culture forever. I saw DC *will* a category-defining business into a billion-dollar outcome. It wasn't tech, it wasn't sales, it wasn't marketing, it wasn't ops: it was culture. Greatness was expected—it was promoted—and mediocrity was not tolerated.

The key to that world-class culture is what I've come to term the Rhythm of Business (RoB). There was a daily, weekly, monthly, quarterly, and annual series of cadences and rituals that defined who we were by what we did. Sunlight was everywhere—there was no hiding in shadows. I'm not exaggerating when I say, done right, this rhythm to Drift was one the most powerful leadership lessons I've ever learned. Our path from a few million in ARR to dozens of millions in ARR happened lightning fast.

At Drift, these were the cadences and rituals to enforce what was promoted and tolerated:

## Daily:

- **Daily Standup:** Every day, every person at the company had to post publicly what they got done yesterday, what they didn't, and what they were working on today in their team's primary channel. Your company doesn't do this? Who cares, I'd advise you to do it anyway. Lead by example.
- **Daily Social Media**: While there was no hard and fast rule that everyone had to post on social media and "learn out loud," as my partner Isaac likes to say, it was the norm for many, and even more of the leadership. They shared stories of customers, learnings from the field, and their opinions on building one of the fastest-growing companies (in revenue) in SaaS history.
- **Daily Product Releases:** One of my favorite things about Drift was that the product shipped code *continuously*. Sure, continuous integration and deployment is no longer a new concept, but watching engineers and product leaders hop on with customers and ship new features or fix bugs daily was a sight to behold. As long as customers asked for it, they got it done. Engineers also sat hand-in-glove with customer support. In fact, customer support reps were called *customer advocates,* and they were embedded directly in the product and engineering teams. DC and Matt Bilotti (employee #3 at Drift) documented some of this development methodology and culture in their brief book *Burndown*. But to witness it first-hand was incredible.

## Weekly:

- **Monday Metrics**: The entire company got together to kick off the week with a review of each department's core metrics.
- **Show & Tell:** The entire company ended the week together with the most fun, unique ritual I've ever been a part of. Every department had three minutes to demonstrate one story of how they shipped something of customer value and upheld the

company leadership principles that week. Every department picked a new team member to represent them every week. And the weekly winner took home the fabled "golden mic," for their department. The goal was to keep the mic in your department each week. It was competitive, it was fun, it was intense—it was a very public (internal) display of what we promoted and what we tolerated. It was my favorite part of working at Drift.

- **Weekly Team Meetings**: Every team had its own cadence of team meetings, which were fast, efficient, effective, and upheld everyone to the standards we professed.

## Monthly:

- **Monthly All-Hands:** This was a monthly kickoff where each department summarized its progress toward quarterly metrics and objectives. These meetings had concrete internal stories backed by data and facts. High standards and customer impact were promoted, and "extreme ownership" (a concept popularized by Navy Seal Jocko Willink in a book that shares the same title) over missing the marks was the only thing that was tolerated. In Executive Leadership Team meetings (ELT), you'd get ripped a new one if you tried to hide behind a story that ignored problems with your side of the business. The company valued extreme ownership and publicly taking your L's almost as much as the wins.
- **Monthly Product Release:** Yep, every month (at our peak) Drift released a new product (or integration). I'm not talking about a new feature; I'm talking about a new product. It was incredible speed, and it was exciting. But this also helped us numerous times release integrations and "powered by" products like Drift Intel that we otherwise would have never been able to release. The entire company rallied behind these releases. Every person in the company would help "launch" these new products in the market, on social media, and with customers and partners. What we promoted was solving for the customer together.

## Quarterly:

- **QBRs and Quarterly Company Review:** There's tons of good content out there about how to run a great QBR. But here's what I can say—these were *stressful*. Why? Because we knew we'd be judged by the truth and nothing but the truth. The preparation and planning were taken seriously, and departments worked together with operations to not just get the insights but also to share the learnings and create the "big rocks" for the next quarter. These were not perfunctory; these were a multi-day part of the cadences and rituals of enforcing what was promoted and what was tolerated. You were expected to come with lessons backed by data—a true story, distilled into insights with a clear plan—or you lost your job. It was that simple.

- **Company and partner events:** We always took our own virtual events and our partner events seriously. Something like this typically happened every month, but every quarter, we would prioritize as a business showing up *in market* wherever our customers and top partners were. When we were the hosts, we'd always be sure to market with the companies our customers already trusted. My favorite moment was during the closing keynote for the Marketo Adobe Summit, delivered by Marketo CEO Steve Lucas. He ended the speech with the words, "...and that's why I'm so proud to announce Conversational ABM with Drift CEO David Cancel."

We closed out the Marketo Adobe Summit in front of an audience of 10,000+ people with the launch of a new co-innovation at their event.

## Annually:

- **Company Kick-off (CKO):** A lot of companies have sales kickoffs (SKOs). Drift had a multi-day *Company* kickoff (CKO) and offsite. Sure, this isn't innovative in and of itself. But it took months to finalize the company's operating model, the logistics, next year's plans, and winning aspirations. We took these very, very seriously.
- **Annual Conference – HYPERGROWTH:** Growing from zero to 1,000 to 6,000 attendees in just two years was a feat in itself for an early-stage startup. But what I loved the most was how we involved partners to make them famous and integrate them with ease. Our (now legendary) VP of Marketing, Dave Gerhardt, deserved a lot of this credit for always being open to what I now refer to as nearbound marketing. But the reality was, it took the whole village.

- **Annual Partner Week:** This was never a *giant* ordeal, and we were never big enough for a partner conference of our own, but we always made it a point to rally the entire company behind a full week where we all showed partners love. We did perfunctory stuff in addition to completely out of this world stuff (including filming a Drift commercial by jumping out of an airplane with our partners Six & Flow). What I loved about partner week is that it was our own small way of reinforcing what we promoted and tolerated, publicly, with our partners.

Is this list comprehensive or perfect? Far from it. However, it emphasizes the point of culture as DC defined it: what you promote, what you tolerate, and the cadences and rituals to enforce them. If you want to establish a strong culture, you need to do the same consistently across every department, every year, quarter, month, week, and day. Clearly define what you promote, what you tolerate, along with the cadences and rituals to enforce them.

## Nearbound Rhythm of Business

If you want to create a nearbound culture, you have to establish the Nearbound Rhythm of Business (RoB). Overlay and weave nearbound into the cadences and rituals of your business, every year, quarter, month, week, and day for every department to drive your company culture instead of your company culture driving you.

Nearbound layers on to every department, but it must be orchestrated by the partnerships team. That means, more than any other role, partner leaders have to learn and understand the rhythms and cadences of the company and each department. To effectively run nearbound plays, partner managers need to be dancing to the same beat as the rest of the org.

The unique challenge of partner pros is that they need to both create their own rhythm of the role and overlay onto the rhythms of others (namely the GTM teams). Here we'll lay out what that might look like.

First, let's explain how to overlay onto the rhythm of another department. Sales typically has the most consistent and robust rhythm, so we're going to use it as the example, but the same applies to marketing and success.

Then, we'll lay out the rhythm of your role and how you can apply those cadences to working with your partners.

Let's break this into chunks, starting with the annual rhythms, and working our way all the way down to daily.

The main thing for the success of your nearbound GTM is for the partner manager to ensure that they are layering partners onto each of the activities and goals of the other departments, in this case, sales. This is where partnerships and operations can work together to create the nearbound overlay.

## The Nearbound Overlay

There are volumes of best practices online for tech, channel, and SaaS businesses when it comes to each of the below activities. For this reason, I'll spare in-depth explanations about each bullet point (e.g., how to run a great annual sales kick-off) and instead encourage you to dive deeper into the collective wisdom of the crowds in communities like Pavilion, Modern Sales Pros, or on websites like SaaStr, who all have more than we could ever read to assist you with any bullet on which you may have a question.

Instead, I'll build each list and add some color or commentary after each when I feel it's needed. Let's start with how to overlay nearbound onto the annual rhythms of the Sales team.

| ANNUALLY | |
|---|---|
| **SALES ACTIVITY** | **WHERE TO LAYER PARTNERSHIPS** |
| **Annual Operating Plan** | Nearbound/Partner Operating Plan |
| Target accounts and segments | Partner overlap on target accounts and segments |
| Territories | Partner presence per territory |
| Unit economics | |
| Revenue targets | Nearbound revenue targets |
| Productivity Per Rep (PPR) | |
| Revenue mix | Partner attach rate |
| **Sales Kick-Off (Sko)** | |

| | |
|---|---|
| Review previous year outcomes and learnings | Outcomes and success stories from last year with partners |
| Align to operating plan, revenue goals, and OKRs | Share attach, velocity, deal size, win rate goals |
| Training and methodologies | Show how to work with you to bring partners into deals |
| New processes and ops | Show any tools used for this (e.g. "Get intro") |
| Comp plans | |
| Cross-departmental announcements | Make a rep who worked with partners a hero! Rep/partner award |

**Notes:** For the annual plan and SKO, partner pros cannot be content to have their own tiny departmental presentation. You have to get CEO and CRO buy-in and bring partner stories into every part of these annual activities. You also have to work closely with operations and finance to ensure the nearbound motion is intertwined into the annual operating plan and models.

**Do not** fall victim to having the CFO try to treat partnerships as a "channel" that has its own tabs abstracted away from the GTM model. There could be a volume unto itself on how to pull this off, but I have to point out this critical piece: don't let partnerships have a cost or production number that is not *a part of* the GTM/sales team. It's one revenue number, not direct and indirect. As discussed in an earlier chapter, one of the best ways to align the teams on this is through Partner Attach Rate (PAR). As Aaron McGarry shared with me in episode #121 of the Nearbound Podcast:

> "If you truly want to have an ecosystem-led go-to-market, attach is the only metric that matters...Reason number one is ecosystem is a team sport. Because if you want, say, 75% partner attach, that means that 75% of marketing activities include our partners. That means 75% of enablement activities include our partners. Just go down the list, right? Every core function of a company has a role to play...
>
> Look at the hyperscalers. What's Google doing? What's Amazon doing? Where are they making investments? What are the announcements they're making? Do you think that Google wants 100% partner attach for fun? No."

The point is simple: unite—don't divide—the partner number. If you're separate, you're old-world "channel." If you're together, you're new world and nearbound.

Tell the story through the lens of sales leadership and the reps—don't take the glory, make them look good! Unite the team to make them the mouthpiece for working with partners. Stories are the key. Having one rep and one partner who can share a success from the previous year will go a long way to excite other reps. You don't want to be the only one sharing the nearbound point of view. Ideally, every session has at least one person you have prepped to bring the nearbound angle to the fore.

Let's move on to the quarterly overlay.

| QUARTERLY | |
|---|---|
| **SALES ACTIVITY** | **WHERE TO LAYER PARTNERSHIPS** |
| **Annual Operating Plan** | Nearbound/Partner Operating Plan |
| Quarterly Business Reviews (QBRs) | *You can't attend every rep QBR but the partner metrics have to be in them all |
| Review previous Q attainment and struggles | Have partner metrics baked into slide template |
| Hold territories and reps accountable to the SKO plan | Are reps/territories hitting their partner attach rates? |
| Reviewing Productivity Per Rep (PPR) | Reviewing Productivity Per Partner and Per Partner Rep |
| Reviewing revenue mix vs goal | Where does nearbound revenue stand (inbound, outbound, nearbound)? |
| Why are people succeeding/struggling? | Specific examples of reps working with/not working with partners |
| Pipeline reviews | Partner source vs. influence |

**Notes**: The key to sales QBRs is preparation. You should have all of the data about which reps and segments worked with partners, what the attach rates were, deal velocity, size, win rate, etc. That requires tight partnership with your operations team to ensure that the leadership, managers, and individual contributors' QBR slide templates always have a space for partner outcomes and data for each group/person.

Your ideal scenario is to have reps saying during the QBR, "I was able to hit quota because I worked with these partners to close these deals," and to have managers saying, "You missed quota, yet you have not attached partners to nearly as many deals as planned. What's going on?"

As my sales mentor, Matt Cameron, taught me, the goal of a QBR is threefold: to educate, inspire, and align.

Educate together with your leadership on what to promote and what you tolerate as a business with nearbound metrics and outcomes on a group and individual contributor (IC) basis.

Inspire others through the words of their peers. That means in IC QBRs, you need to have reps who inspire other reps with their own stories. The same should be said for managers or leadership QBRs. If a territory is crushing because of a leader who's managing her team to nearbound motions, she better dang well be inspiring the other leaders to step up or fall behind.

And lastly, align. Are people pacing toward the annual number on their revenue mix from pipeline, closed-won revenue, partner assists, and attach rate? Where did they perform vs. their quarterly numbers?

Let's tackle monthly sales rhythms next.

| MONTHLY | |
|---|---|
| **SALES ACTIVITY** | **WHERE TO LAYER PARTNERSHIPS** |
| Monthly sales all hands | *Get agenda ahead of time and send partner data for each rep |
| Celebrate top performers and wins | Stories of top reps working with partners |
| Track against quarterly targets | Each rep/segment needs to have partner attach included |
| | Every slide needs partner #s, AND you need your own slide for partner performance for the entire sales team to see |
| Enablement team meeting | *Ensure partnerships are part of every enablement session |

**Notes**: Like other cadences and rituals before the monthly cadence, quality comes from preparation. You have to have done the work to have proof before you can showcase it. And, just as importantly, you must prepare with operations and sales leadership to ensure those key wins and anecdotes are told through the voices of those who are working *with* partners in your sales org. Your goal here is yet again simple but not easy: it's not about your talk time about partners, it's about *your sales team's* talk time about partners. Make them the voice in these meetings. From your CRO to sales enablement, down to an AE who's winning with nearbound plays.

On to weekly rhythms.

| **WEEKLY** | |
|---|---|
| **SALES ACTIVITY** | **WHERE TO LAYER PARTNERSHIPS** |
| Forecast Meeting | |
| | Identify at-risk opportunities and where partners can help |
| | Discuss any deals where partners made it worse. |
| | Partner forecast number |
| Pipeline Meeting | |
| | Partners that create pipeline should get partner attach. Highlight partners who have assisted with intel, influence, or intros to open up pipeline and dial in the partners who *should* be tapped into for later-stage deals or customer accounts when they are sourcing. "Partner sourced," for better or worse, probably isn't going away for some time. Make sure you reward those partners in front of the sales and account management teams every week. Highlight them, and make them famous internally with reps. |

**Notes**: The rubber really meets the road in the weekly RoB. If a partner leader is not a core part of—and attending—the weekly pipeline and forecast meetings, then you're nowhere near where you need to be. These two rituals are critical to almost every business: Pipeline that's opened (and the progress to pipeline creation targets and methods on a per-rep basis) and pipeline that's supposed to close by a certain time (aka forecast). Typically, these two standard meetings are run at both a leadership and per rep or team level. And in later-stage or public companies, that weekly forecast call is something that is escalated to the entire C-suite and board.

In the nearbound overlay model, your goal is to bake in the partner metrics, anecdotes, and levers for further partner involvement as part of the dashboards or templates used by the sales team overall, or in each sales segment, if you've grown to a size where these are rolled up into one final weekly pipeline and forecast report to the business. If you're not working closely with operations here to bake this into the RoB, you're not nearbound. You'll just be another number on a spreadsheet.

Finally, let's hit the daily rhythms.

## DAILY

| SALES ACTIVITY | WHERE TO LAYER PARTNERSHIPS |
|---|---|
| Dashboards | Dashboards |
| 1-1 meetings | |
| Demos/calls/emails | Tags, filters, and alerts for movement on deals with partner presence or potential overlap. |
| | Prep reps with any partner intel on accounts |
| Living in CRM and with buyers | Ensure partner presence visible where reps live |

**Notes:** My sales mentor of nearly a decade, Matt Cameron, over-indexes on the power of front-line management. In other words, not just executive competency, and alignment to the motions of the business, but managers who have a pod of quota carrying reps directly reporting to them. Managers are often promoted to these positions without any coaching or history as a manager. Here's what I can say about front-line management: your nearbound RoB for sales *will* come down to the degree to which your managers are competent, confident, and coaching to nearbound metrics, objectives, and plays on a daily basis.

Matt once told me that managers (alongside operations) must always "inspect what you expect." What a quote. If managers are not inspecting for partner involvement, how could you possibly ever *expect* it? Ensure that your leadership and operations team are setting up front-line management for success with the proper visibility on both the team and per-rep basis where they live—*their* dashboards and reports, not yours. You can't coach every play on the sales team. Heck, managers barely can even when they're good. Make managers good, damn good, at inspecting and coaching for partner involvement if you want great outcomes.

## The Rhythm of the Partnerships Role

In addition to layering onto sales and other departments, you have to establish your own rhythm for partnerships—you might even refer to this as *internal* vs *external*. What activities are you doing with your team, and what are you doing with partners on a regular cadence?

I've broken down the basics of a nearbound rhythm of the role into checklists. This is how I frame the major activities for each time segment, starting annually and working down to daily. It's not exhaustive or fully explained; I provide them here to give you a starting point. Stay curious—if something here doesn't make sense, go find someone in the partner ecosystem who has done it before.

### Annual Nearbound Partnerships Rhythm

- ☐ Align with company/each department kick-off
- ☐ Align with each department and company operating plan
- ☐ Understand your partner book/ecosystem; know the current state
    - ☐ How many partners are attached/ partner attach rate on a unit/segment basis?
    - ☐ How many partners are overlapped? What's the nearbound opportunity?
    - ☐ What does "good" look like? Prep for enablement, training, and coaching.
- ☐ Where you landed in your numbers last year
    - ☐ Marketing

- [ ] Pipeline sourced/influenced from partners, co-marketing, nearbound marketing, and attach to marketing campaigns
        - [ ] Revenue
            - [ ] Partner attach to pipeline and closed-won broken down by sourced, influenced, and on a per-partner basis
        - [ ] Success
            - [ ] Gross and net retention with partner attach
        - [ ] Product
            - [ ] What did your company ship with partners, what are the stories, and what was the customer impact?
            - [ ] Data on what companies influence your target account list or install base
            - [ ] Who do you need to add as new partners to your target partner list?
- [ ] Setting your goals for # of partners, new partners, active partners, attach, etc.
- [ ] What does the partner book look like on a per rep basis
    - [ ] How many partners?
    - [ ] What segments?
    - [ ] What type of partners? Tech, service, etc.
- [ ] What's your partner value prop?
    - [ ] Why would they want to partner with you? What's in it for them? Remember, not all partner value is the same
- [ ] Program design - adjust to company OKRs
    - [ ] Tiering
    - [ ] Comp
    - [ ] Agreements
    - [ ] Process
    - [ ] Measurement and reporting back to partners (reduce cycles between feedback loops and don't overly rely on PRM or portals that partners have a hard time logging back into)
- [ ] Target partners
    - [ ] Create and review an annual plan with them
        - [ ] E.g. "How we exceed the $500k benchmark this year"
- [ ] Top partners (3-5)

- [ ] Exec-to-exec alignment, not just partner managers talking to partner managers; get your and their leadership talking—and I *do* mean direct leadership (nearbound, baby)
- [ ] Top target partners
    - [ ] Must align with the operating model and target accounts/regions/industry/company size, etc.
    - [ ] Do the partners you have get you the deals you want? Who would? Who is working with the customers you want not just the customers you have?
- [ ] Partner Kick-off event
- [ ] Create your budget
    - [ ] Tech stack
    - [ ] Headcount
    - [ ] Events - your own and partner events
    - [ ] Partner marketing budget for recruitment
    - [ ] Nearbound marketing budget for co-marketing
    - [ ] Show incremental gains on the operating plan, not just how the partner will contribute to what's already happening
- [ ] Dashboards, internal overlap data, the scope of ecosystem and nearbound network.

**Notes**: In general, these *external* items are not altogether that different from the cadences and rituals of your internal RoB. The principle is this: if you are going to live, build, and win in-market with the network of people who surround your customers, then you must have an equal quality of rhythm for those external parties. Your goal is to unite not only the folks within the walls of your company, but also the parties your customers already trust. Be intentional on an annual basis. Your strategy is a choice. Make sure your partners and the nearbound network understand those choices as clearly and as plainly as possible.

## Quarterly Nearbound Partnerships Rhythm

- [ ] Partner QBRs (with top 3-10 partners per partner manager)
    - [ ] Key wins/losses, learnings, targets + accounts
    - [ ] Product updates, launches, and releases both ways
    - [ ] Bring in key executives internally and externally to each other's QBRs. Executive alignment isn't just a buzzword. These QBRs are a forcing function to bring your other departmental leaders into your partner's businesses.

- [ ] Pro-tip: Appoint each executive on your team 3-5 partners where they play executive sponsor for the year and get their commitment to joining each quarterly QBR. Remember, cadences and rituals are the backbone of culture. QBRs are a perfect forcing function.
- [ ] Play a role in other dept QBRs
    - [ ] Bring your partners into internal circles when they can make an impact, and make sure you are present in *their* QBRs, not just them in yours. You already did the work if you have a QBR with a partner. Take those lessons and insights into theirs. It's time well spent.
- [ ] QBR for all PMs
    - [ ] Have they moved the needle?
    - [ ] Reviewing partner manager dashboard for attainment of OKRs, book review, and internal QBRs.
    - [ ] Are they ready for their external QBRs with partners? Your internal partner manager QBRs need to happen *before* the external partner QBRs.

**Notes**: Again, the key to these meetings is preparation. You should have the data prepared and be ready to tell the story of both high-level impact over the quarter for both companies, and the individual plays and collaborations between you and your partner reps that worked together. This allows you to not only highlight wins but also replicate the plays that brought them together.

## Monthly Nearbound Partnerships Rhythm

- [ ] Meetings with the top 20% of partners on:
    - [ ] Updates, product releases, markets, etc.
    - [ ] Success stories/examples/feedback loops
    - [ ] Review nearbound account lists
    - [ ] 3x5 matrix play (as discussed in the *Nearbound Sales Blueprint* chapter)
    - [ ] Pipe/forecast with partner. What does each partner's book and funnel look like on a per-account basis?
    - [ ] Bring Reveal data on new overlaps (both directions)
        - [ ] For example, give updates like, "We are about to close these three big logos."
        - [ ] Use 360° mapping to give visibility

- ☐ Attend each top partner's critical monthly meetings
- ☐ Meetings with partners' department heads
    - ☐ Overlaying to their staff
    - ☐ Give partners' specific executives and key stakeholders facetime to share stories of working with you
        - ☐ Make partner and internal reps famous
    - ☐ Reviewing numbers and outcomes

**Notes**: Don't over-index on your dashboards and reports with your partners in your monthly meetings. The truth is that they will never log in to your portal as much as you think they will, or you'd like them to. This cadence is about prepping for the meetings, the time with the partner, identifying patterns and impact, and the top-to-bottom alignment for both teams.

## Weekly Partnerships Rhythm

- ☐ Sales meetings
- ☐ Review overlaps
    - ☐ New overlaps
    - ☐ Stuck deals
    - ☐ Automated Slack, Teams, or email notifications
- ☐ Partner account and opportunity reviews—look at the funnel of activities and next steps. What accounts are waiting on a next step and from what partner? Create action lists for aging activities and accounts.
    - ☐ Reveal pipeline and collaboration views
    - ☐ Write emails for other people
        - ☐ AEs
        - ☐ Partners
        - ☐ Pro-tip: Get great at helping reps write emails for partners for intel, influence, and intros and schedule meetings. Get things moving.
- ☐ Run nearbound plays and document the activities and dispositions
    - ☐ Ensure statuses are up to date on open and review aging activities waiting on you, your reps, or partners. This is your partner activity dashboard.
        - ☐ Pro-tip: Check out *The Ultimate Guide to Driving Revenue with Nearbound Sales* for step-by-step

guidance on how to best update partner activities and dispositions.
- [ ] Set up filters on call intelligence tools like Clari, Gong and in CRM for words like "partner," "agency," "integration," key partner company names, etc.
    - [ ] Use to find new partners and partner types
    - [ ] Use to track influence
- [ ] Ensure partner attach metric is up to date
    - [ ] Giving credit where due
    - [ ] Get AE/CS/AM approval for partner attach and document the supporting activities
    - [ ] Communicate back to partner—always close the feedback loop
- [ ] Look for opportunities to help partners close deals (remember the first helper principle)
    - [ ] Their ops to your customers
    - [ ] Review the 3x5 strategy account lists
    - [ ] Bring intel, influence, and intros from your CSMs/AEs
    - [ ] Account reviews with CSMs on accounts in need of saving or expansion (internal)
        - [ ] Partner managers bring intel to partners proactively
        - [ ] These are surfaced in the weekly partner manager cadences and then in the partner meetings themselves
    - [ ] Seed vs. sow
        - [ ] Document your help and log it to be used in your upcoming QBR
        - [ ] For example, "Here's the assist I gave you with 3 I's for X account."
- [ ] Weekly syncs with top partners (or async via Slack, Teams, or email) using a weekly partner meeting template

**Notes**: Weekly meetings with top partners are where you ensure that the activities on specific accounts and initiatives have completed their outstanding next steps. These weekly syncs are your best feedback loops for coaching your partner reps in your 1-1s. These are the calls partner leaders need to inspect and coach against in their 1-1s with their frontline partner managers. Remember that the improvements, results, and actions discussed in the meetings should be accumulated for your partner manager QBRs.

## Daily Nearbound Partnerships Rhythm

- ☐ Dashboard/funnel for partner manager 1-1s
    - ☐ CRM, PRM, and Reveal for movement in the field
    - ☐ Create two separate updates, one for partners and one for internal nearbound activity and play progress. See *The Ultimate Guide to Driving Revenue with Nearbound Sales* for more guidance: https://nearbound.com/resources/the-nearbound-guide/
    - ☐ Review current pipeline/deals
- ☐ Calendar review: What does the week look like?
- ☐ To-do review: Which of the 10 tasks for the week am I doing today?
- ☐ Comms review
    - ☐ SMS or call: If you aren't texting and calling daily with your top partners, you're not breaking through. Don't rely on portals.
    - ☐ Slack/Teams updates: These are subservient to the phone, but are often required for lengthier context and information sharing
    - ☐ Email: The third most effective, but often required for certain partner communications
- ☐ Close the loop before closing the laptop
    - ☐ Your top partners should always know what happened that day, and what tomorrow's to-do list is

**Notes:** Remember, nearbound is about uniting the company around the people and partners your customers already trust. You have to become a master of keeping everyone up to date. The "orchestrator" analogy may seem trite, but the reality is that you can't help call plays across your partners and the field if you're not watching the game and communicating. Always close the loop—don't make partners wait on you and coach front-line partner managers on the plays they are calling. Be a chief communicator and always circle back. Reduce the cycles between feedback loops to win at the nearbound rhythm of the role.

Creating a nearbound culture is bigger than educating yours and your partners' companies on the importance and power of nearbound GTM. It's far bigger than setting up workflows and initiatives. Your sales team doesn't want new workflows and more work. But what they do want is help. Nearbound culture is about understanding the ways your and your partners' teams are working, the goals they are working towards, the places they are working in, and integrating your nearbound strategy into the daily, weekly, monthly, quarterly, and annual actions that make up these rhythms. Make seeking help through nearbound second nature to those you are working alongside, and watch the growth happen in real-time.

The Nearbound Rhythm of Business, along with your Rhythm of the Role, dictates what you promote and tolerate, as well as the cadences and rituals necessary to instill it. If you're not running your business this way, your business will run you. Take hold of the wheel and be the leader your company needs you to be. Is it easy? Hardly. Leadership is never easy, but if you embrace the right mindset, you can discover the curiosity that powers courage, and the courage to find your conviction.

## CHAPTER 15

# THE NEARBOUND MINDSET

At 211 degrees, water is hot. At 212 degrees, it boils. With boiling water comes steam, and with steam, you can power a train. This transformation hinges on a one-degree shift—a tiny nudge that unleashes previously impossible power. This is how all great change starts: unnoticed at first until the boundaries of what's possible are redrawn.

The ancient Greek philosopher Polybius had a term for the cyclical progression and regression of political regimes and leadership throughout history: *Anakyklosis*. Also called the Polybian Cycle, it's the dance of recycled societal paradigms. The cycle is best summarized by G. Michael Hopf's oft-quoted passage from *Those Who Remain*:

> *Hard times create strong leaders.*
>
> *Strong leaders create good times.*
>
> *Good times create weak leaders.*
>
> *And weak leaders create hard times.*

Within the crucible of hard times, strong leaders are forged. They boil the waters of their time, one degree at a time, and pave the way to good times once more.

This ebb and flow, though timeless, isn't predestined. It's driven by minor changes, subtle shifts in thinking, and, sometimes, the actions of a few people. Just as one degree can shift the state of water, a handful of individuals can determine the direction of an era. As an American revolutionary once said, *"It does not take a majority to prevail, but rather an irate, tireless minority, keen on setting brushfires of freedom in the minds of [all]."*

Irate, tireless, and keen. Samuel Adams didn't choose those words lightly.

But with each new historical revolution of the Polybian Cycle, the stakes seem to get larger. The hard times we're in are so much harder because of how good they've been in recent memory. At the same time, the next turning is more ripe with potential than we can imagine.

**The future is here in medicine:** Consider the advancement of organic multicellular robots—*Anthrobots*—that have turned science fiction into reality. These entities, crafted from human lung tissue, boast the ability to move autonomously, survive up to two months, and possess capabilities for healing wounds and repairing neural tissue. The potential applications appear limitless, yet they remain tantalizingly out of reach.

**The future is here in energy:** We hear rumors of fusing atoms and sustained fusion reactors. Despite these advances, the power grid remains vulnerable, and nuclear fusion has been "ten years away" for decades.

**The future is here in transportation:** SpaceX is aiming rocket ships at Mars, and autonomous vehicles are starting to populate the streets of various cities. And yet, the idea of a Mars colony still feels remote, and most of us aren't ready to let go of the steering wheel.

**The future is here in finance:** Amid the growing buzz and excitement over cryptocurrencies and AI-driven financial advisories, there is an equal amount of anxiety around the rise of financial surveillance, artificial superintelligence, and resistance to dollar hegemony. Money will never be the same, someday.

And last but not least…

**The future is here in partnerships:** We're told that it has arrived. I've said so myself. We see collaborations that are redefining boundaries, signaling a future where connectedness becomes the norm, and the best entrepreneurs build *in* the market, instead of just going *to* market. Yet, partnership departments continue to play second fiddle to other departments. Are we—partnership leaders, new-era entrepreneurs, and change agents—part of that irate, tireless minority keen on setting brushfires to set us free from the confines of the old world? Will our waters hit the critical temperature of 212 degrees? Or will our visions simmer silently?

The future, with all its promise and challenges, feels both immediately within reach and yet distant—a paradox that defines our time.

What explains this dichotomy? Why does every leap forward seem tethered? Why does progress feel both dizzyingly rapid and painstakingly slow? And why do we feel this tension deeper today than ever before?

Perhaps it's because we intuit that the forces of good and evil, innovation and stagnation, freedom and control, are both capable of winning. The future will be shaped by today's leaders. The question is, where do we stand, and have we made our choice with conviction?

Being a leader today is both thrilling and daunting. The potential for impact is immense, yet the responsibility it carries brings the risk of significant mistakes. Doubt often creeps in, fueled by fears of unintended consequences or the inertia of the status quo. At times, we find ourselves hesitating, unsure of our next step.

Weak leadership can deepen crises, typically by fostering division over unity. This "divide and conquer" approach may offer short-term gains, but ultimately, it benefits no one. Such tactics are not only ineffective but also detrimental to our collective well-being. We're capable of much more and deserve leaders who recognize that.

Strong leaders use their power to bridge divides. They channel the transformative potential of the times towards outcomes, not egos. Ego is worthless, but outcomes are valuable. The time for exceptional leadership is not in some distant future — it's right now.

## The Power Law Revisited

In the late 19th century, Vilfredo Pareto—a political economist—made an astute observation that would forever etch his name into the annals of economic theory. As he tended to his garden, Pareto was struck by the fact that just 20% of the peapods he nurtured yielded 80% of the peas. He began noticing this 80/20 pattern elsewhere.

20% of the Italian population owned 80% of the land.

20% of the companies earned 80% of the profits.

This pattern, which soon evolved into the renowned *Pareto Principle*, is evident far beyond garden beds and Italian estates. Many of us find that 20% of our daily effort is often responsible for 80% of our most significant achievements (think Cal Newport's *Deep Work*).

Today, the "80/20" rule is polarizing the world into two camps: those who leverage technology and those left in its wake. As economist Tyler Cowen notes, the age where "average" was good enough is gone. High achievers are propelled even higher by technological leverage, while the average among us find their foothold slipping.

In the realm of social media, a small group of influencers enjoys the majority of followers and revenue. Only 1% of YouTube accounts have crossed the 100-subscriber threshold, while MrBeast has 181 million subscribers. Similarly, in the eCommerce sector, a few giants like Amazon overshadow countless smaller retailers struggling to survive.

As we venture further into an age dominated by technology, a select few—even fewer than the proverbial 20%—who wield these tools with finesse will reap rewards far surpassing their modest numbers. They'll command more than their anticipated 80%, altering economies and reshaping organizational structures in ways previously unimaginable.

Are you willing to be the 20%?

I don't want to sound too dramatic, but stick with me here. The shift to a nearbound mindset follows the same distribution. It is one that most probably won't make, but the minority who do will reap outsized returns.

For many, this book and mindset will be a handy tool—a playbook of strategies to dabble with. You might tweak a tactic here and there, close a few more deals, fortify a handful of partnerships, and bask in the glow of short-lived success. Then life will sweep you back into its familiar rhythm.

But some of you—maybe 20%—will feel an intense and even unnerving realization of destiny—a personal conviction so deep it echoes Paul Atreides's "terrible purpose" in Dune. I warned you it might sound dramatic, but your life really is a grand adventure with dragons to slay and people to rescue. It's not just business. It's life—your life.

Once you take the partner pill and shift into nearbound thinking, your perception of leadership, partnerships, and business strategy will shift, and your life will never be the same again. This gravitational pull towards transformation won't require luck. It's not about chance; it's about choice.

If this sentiment resonates, I'm writing especially for you.

## Back to the Future: From How to Who

Throughout this book, I've come back to the pivotal shift from the How Economy to the Who Economy, highlighting the pressing challenges and opportunities this transition presents for every business venture.

I've aimed to elevate the role of partnerships from just another department—often sidelined on organizational charts—to a crucial, all-encompassing strategy across all departments—**nearbound**. But while strategies, tactics, and plans are vital, one element stands out: leadership.

Ask yourself: *who* in your company is leading the overlay model of partnerships across all fronts?

In our exploration, we have looked closely at how different teams contribute to this model, such as:

- **Marketing:** Where you live in the market and market *with* your partners.
- **Sales:** Where partnerships and networks open new channels to kickstart the flywheel of revenue through intel, influence, and intros.
- **Success:** Where the flywheel is accelerated, and a program becomes an ecosystem.
- **Operations:** Where network effects and partnerships are overlaid into the rhythms of every team, not merely bolted onto the company as a business unit, channel, or department.

Each department or team, working with partners, can hasten your company's metamorphosis into the Nearbound Era.

But you still need leaders in your C-Suite to champion the cause of partnerships with conviction beyond just meeting revenue targets with partners.

**HubSpot** is a prime example. While founders Brian Halligan and Dharmesh Shah are celebrated for their visionary leadership, it was the robust ecosystem they cultivated that propelled HubSpot into a multi-billion-dollar business. Their partner programs were never peripheral; they were fundamental, championed by leaders who believed deeply in embedding partnerships into the company's core.

Similarly, the success of **Salesforce's** AppExchange goes beyond its groundbreaking products; it embodies a profound understanding of partnership dynamics. This marketplace has evolved into an expansive ecosystem, thanks in large part to leaders who viewed partnerships not as supplementary but as essential to Salesforce's identity.

Across industries, a pattern emerges: while founders and core teams lay the groundwork, there often arises within these ecosystems a pivotal figure—a true partner leader, who reshapes the company's trajectory and, by extension, sets new benchmarks for the industry. These visionaries extend the reach of their departments, infusing the spirit of partnership throughout the organizational fabric.

As you ponder your company's future direction and your personal leadership journey, consider not just the *how* but the *who*. Who will be your beacon, leading you into this new era of boundless partnership potential?

Will it be you?

## The Three C's of the Nearbound Mindset

Reflecting on our journey through this book, we arrive at a pivotal point. Leadership in the Nearbound Era is not just about strategies or departmental success; it's about embodying a mindset that drives change.

I recall a defining moment, seated in a Sequoia-backed boardroom across from industry giants. The weight of their expectations was palpable. They awaited answers I was expected to provide on forging successful partnerships, yet I faced a daunting realization: there was no playbook or established methodology for navigating the complexities of SaaS and hyper-growth startups in the realm of partnerships.

This epiphany underscored a critical truth: transformation within companies isn't spearheaded by titles or departments, but by individuals who embody the nearbound mindset. These leaders, like entrepreneurs within an existing firm, are distinguished not merely by their willingness to innovate or appetite for risks but by their unwavering vision.

What sets these individuals apart is their embodiment of the Three C's:

- Curiosity
- Courage
- Conviction

This triad forms the core of the nearbound mindset. Their path is not defined by following the footsteps of others but by carving out new ones, driven by a deep-seated belief in their vision and the transformative potential of partnerships.

**Curiosity** is the initial spark. It's the relentless drive that Jeff Bezos describes as the "day zero mentality"—a quest for the unknown, tackling challenges head-on, and delving deep into complexities that deter others. Many are content at the edge of discovery, satisfied with a superficial understanding. However, the nearbound mindset is fueled by a curious obsession with the market, the customer, and their ecosystem, seeking to uncover layers beyond the obvious.

**Courage** follows. More than bravery, it's the audacity to step into the unknown and make decisive choices, even when it means forgoing many options to place your bet. Courage means facing potential failures with a defiant smile, ready to confront whatever comes.

**Conviction** transcends both curiosity and courage. It's a virtue found in the rarest of leaders. It's not just a guiding principle but a force that draws others in and propels its holder with relentless momentum. When you have conviction, you are willing to "die on that hill," consequences be damned.

Together, Curiosity, Courage, and Conviction comprise a powerful trifecta essential for anyone aiming for true transformation.

## Curiosity

My curiosity about nearbound began with an unremarkable Zoom call. On the other side sat my mentor, Pete Caputa, with the Boston Commons stretching out behind me—a view from Drift's boardroom. We were in the midst of our monthly advisory meeting, and I was prodding for insights on replicating HubSpot's dynamic partner ecosystem and alignment. Essentially, I was seeking Pete's secrets to forging a world-class partnerships department. As my gaze wandered over the virtual Boston backdrop, Pete's words cut through my distraction.

"Jared, this isn't just about the channel or partnerships department," he clarified. "**It's about an overlay model.**" An overlay model? What the heck was Pete talking about?

That moment marked a turning point when it dawned on me that partnerships should not be confined to a single department but integrated as a strategy across *every* department. The concept of an overlay model ignited my curiosity, setting me on a path of discovery that has spanned six years and counting.

Driven by this newfound obsession, I decided to seek out leaders who had successfully dismantled the traditional barriers—not only aligning their leadership with partnerships but also weaving these partnerships into the very fabric of their departments. My quest for knowledge led me to launch *PartnerUp: The Partnerships Podcast*. Initially, my motivation was pure curiosity, without any anticipation of it becoming the leading podcast in the field.

Soon, my curiosity paved the way for the creation of PartnerHacker with Isaac Morehouse, a longtime friend turned co-founder. Together, we initiated PartnerHacker Daily—the first daily newsletter dedicated to partnerships—and assembled the best-selling PartnerHacker Handbook. Our efforts culminated in hosting the PL[X] Summit, the largest event in B2B tech partnerships history, attracting over 5,000 attendees, eventually leading to our acquisition by Reveal, where PartnerHacker was rebranded to nearbound.com. Without curiosity, you wouldn't be reading this book.

## Courage

Curiosity is one thing, but for many people, that's where the journey ends. Had I not found some courage, we never could have helped kickstart the "moment partnerships go mainstream."

For Pete, curiosity had been the launchpad for testing the thesis that would form many components of a nearbound strategy—his building of HubSpot's agency program that I introduced at the beginning of this book.

Recall that before Pete joined HubSpot as one of its first 20 employees, he was already immersed in the agency world—nurturing a growing curiosity about the transformative potential of technology and content marketing for agencies. At HubSpot, he began selling to agencies until the CEO Brian Halligan, told him to stop, citing concerns about the agencies' high churn rate not aligning with HubSpot's ideal customer profile.

When the CEO tells you to stop something in as many words, what do you do? You stop.

Well, it's not what Pete did. He didn't stop selling to agencies. *The guts!*

Pete knew the risk of going against his CEO, it meant he could very well lose his job. Still, with some light support from HubSpot legend and manager Dan Tyre, he pushed forward from curiosity to courage. The outcome?

He quadrupled his sales quota in a single quarter. His efforts laid the foundation for what became a $100M agency program, the likes of which HubSpot had never seen.

Ultimately, Pete's strategy not only proved successful but also challenged the CEO's initial reservations, showcasing the tangible impact of courage through remarkable results and revenue.

And the very CEO who told him "No" was proven wrong by a measurable result: revenue.

Looking at HubSpot today, you might assume its partnership-centric ethos was planned from the start by its founders. By all means, Brian Halligan and Dharmesh Shah are some of the greatest founders in SaaS history. However, the truth reveals a different architect behind its agency success. It was Pete's willingness to embrace risk for what he believed was right that not only transformed HubSpot but also made a lasting imprint on the marketing industry.

If you didn't know this story, you would assume looking at HubSpot today that their partner friendliness and world-class agency program was the product of intentional planning by co-founders Brian and Dharmesh.

Pete's journey from a curious innovator to a courageous leader, and now the CEO of Databox illustrates the essence of the nearbound mindset.

He embodies the rare blend of curiosity and courage that reshaped an industry.

## Conviction

Before launching PartnerHacker, I didn't have the conviction of someone with Pete's track record. It was something I borrowed from another mentor, Bobby Napiltonia, whose story needs telling.

Bobby, as Salesforce's SVP of worldwide Partnerships under CEO Marc Benioff, was instrumental in the early development of what has become a trillion-dollar ecosystem. Bobby helped propel the launch of the largest marketplace in B2B SaaS, the Salesforce App Exchange, in addition to minting some of the largest GSI and tech partnerships in history—including Accenture and Salesforce. But Salesforce wasn't Bobby's first rodeo—he wasn't there to take orders or simply "run" the partner department. He was playing to win, consequences be damned.

From day one, Salesforce was a "cloud platform" for CRM, but it wasn't always what you thought it was. Whenever Salesforce went public in 2004, guess what the average number of seats per account was.

100? 200? 300?

Try seven.

Bobby *knew* that it was going to take an ecosystem to grow.

Pete's defiance against Brian Halligan's directive at HubSpot showcased courage, a daring move to validate the importance of partnerships. But Bobby's approach with Benioff transcended courage; it was grounded in an unshakeable belief in the essential role of partnerships within Salesforce's narrative. He didn't see it as taking a risk; for him, it was a matter of conviction.

Bobby's conviction led him to present Benioff with what was essentially an ultimatum: unless partnerships were elevated to one of the company's top three values—and publicly championed by Benioff himself—he was prepared to walk away and take the team with him. Bobby wasn't seeking personal acclaim or challenging the CEO for the sake of it; he was ensuring that the ethos of partnering with customers would be woven into Salesforce's DNA, not as a departmental task but as a company-wide mandate.

Bobby's stance was clear: without the CEO's direct endorsement of partnerships, this job held little value to him. He insisted that if Benioff truly aimed to succeed through partnerships, then he needed to lead this charge, ensuring that Salesforce's culture and operations universally embraced partnerships as a core value, not relegated to a single department. Bobby didn't just suggest; he convinced Benioff that "partner success" wasn't the job of one department, *it was the job of every department*.

I'm sure there was plenty of grace, a business case, and deep texture to this conversation. Furthermore, Benioff had been partner-friendly. But can you imagine going up to Marc Benioff—*the* Marc Benioff—with such an ultimatum if you were merely curious about partnerships? Even with courage, you'd be lying to yourself if you think you would do this without true conviction.

**That** is the nearbound mindset.

## The Call to Action

When you embody the three C's the focus shifts from individual leadership to collective action. You're no longer the centerpiece. Instead, your role is to immerse yourself in the buyer's ecosystem and empower and assist everyone else.

Although I've emphasized the importance of the P&L and putting W's on the board, that's table stakes. Don't ignore the data, but treat these metrics as the output, not the input. They are the rearview mirror, not the windshield. You have more leverage to change the fundamentals of your outputs through the inputs of the market.

How much of your time is spent *in market*? We spend far more time thinking about *how* to run our businesses than about *who* surrounds our customers and the changes in the market. But buyers couldn't give a damn about your Go-To-Market strategy. They don't care about emails, ads, or product marketing.

Buyers care about the people who have already been to the places they are trying to go. They care about who is helping them reach their promised land. Your customers don't care how you do it, but they do care *who* you do it with. Your customers care that you earn the trust of those around them. They care about who.

So let me ask you the question: if it's not you who will lead this charge at your company, who will? The status quo cannot stand. The inertia of siloed departments, the tyranny of the familiar, and the maddening state of GTM will not change by itself.

It can only change through you. The few who are curious, courageous, and fearless in their convictions. The few who are committed to not just running another company or heading a department but charting a new course for their market and their customers.

Go forth and help your marketing team; market together.
Go forth and help your sales team; sell together.
Go forth and help your customer success team; serve together.
Go forth and help your product team; build together
Go forth and help your operations team; work together.

The evidence is overwhelming, the plays are abundant, and the resources are at your fingertips. You have this book and the best ecosystem in all of tech: the partner ecosystem.

May your curiosity lead you to courage, and may your convictions strengthen your choices.

A nearbound leader, no matter their role, is the most powerful unifying force within an organization. They toss aside the shackles of ivory tower intellectualism to champion the company's ultimate mission: ensuring customer success within their ecosystem.

Unite your company around the customer, surround them with partners, and change the course of your market forever.

## ABOUT THE AUTHOR

Jared Fuller is the Chief Ecosystem Officer at Reveal and the Co-founder of nearbound.com. He is the editor of the best-selling *PartnerHacker Handbook*, host of The Nearbound Podcast, and a prolific speaker and writer on partnerships and Go-To-Market strategies.

Jared has led partnerships and sales teams at two unicorns, founded multiple startups, and has been kicked out of at least one casino for winning too much at the blackjack table

# ABOUT NEARBOUND.COM

nearbound.com is the #1 place for the principles, tactics, and trends in nearbound GTM. The Nearbound Daily newsletter, articles, podcasts, and events highlight and shape the best conversations from the best minds in B2B. Subscribe for free at nearbound.com and join the revolution!

# ABOUT REVEAL.CO

Reveal is the Nearbound Revenue Platform that brings partner data into your CRM so you can leverage intel, influence, and intros from those your buyers trust. Try it free at reveal.co.

Printed in Great Britain
by Amazon